Comfortable Madness
William L. Alton

© 2018 William L. Alton

Edition
10 9 8 7 6 5 4 3 2 1

ISBN
978-0-9973988-9-2

Credits
Cover: ProDesign

Hibernian Publishing, LLC
New Jersey

Dedication

To Jennifer and Julie. Two sides of the same coin.

Hush

I was eighteen. I was dreaming. At least, I thought I was dreaming. I was in a large room. A room so large it had no walls or windows. No shadows or corners. Everything was smooth and hard, the color of fresh bruises.

There was music and I danced. I danced like I'd never danced in the real world. When I jumped, I jumped so high I forgot about gravity. I spun and crouched. Music flowed through me like light through an old, yellow window. It was fantastic.

But then, he was there. His hands found my hips, warm and strong. They lifted me up. His chest pressed against my spine and it never occurred to me to be shy about my nudity. It was as natural as water in a creek. We spun and leapt and I never saw his face.

"Hush," he said. "This is a secret."

Every piece of me trembled. The world changed. He lay with me on my bed. His strong hands stroked me, cupped me and held me. Lips crawled down my belly to my thighs. He pressed his lips to the back of my neck, too hot, too dry to be anything other than a brand. Still, I turned to water. Fire burned along my ribs. My thighs quivered and twitched. It was neither pleasant nor distasteful. There was no frame of reference.

Part of me jerked away and tried to wake. Part of me spun in his arms and waited. That's when the dream changed. I was not in the vast empty room. I was on my bed, in my room and he was there, pushing into me.

Pain arced along my spine and my innards exploded. I screamed. I cried. I twisted and jerked. Nothing made it stop. Nothing made it better. He filled me with pain and madness and shame. For a moment, I was dead but then I rose again.

"Hush," he said.

I reached for his face, but it was dark and all I saw were cheekbones, the bridge of his nose.

Somehow, it ended. The light changed, and the walls came into focus. Tayla said my name. Suddenly light filled the room and my eyes watered.

"Butter?" Tayla said. "Butter."

I lay on the bed and shivered. Cold air pressed against my sweaty skin and I couldn't move. Tayla pressed her fingertips to my face. I jerked and screamed.

"Butter," she said. "It's a nightmare."

A nightmare. It was a nightmare and more than a nightmare. Nightmares always sank like water into sand when I woke. This, this one stayed with me. I remembered his chest's broad, hard plane, his jaw's chiseled edges. The smell of myrrh filled the room and I knew it was the man from my dream. Somehow, I knew my life had changed. I didn't know how or why, but it had changed and there was no going back.

Lines

Mornings sucked. Anxiety poisoned everything. Yesterday's anxiety. Today's. Tomorrow's. I lay in my bed, frozen and sad, watching pale blue streamers run from wall to wall. Everything was misty and kind of shiny. Pretty and frightening all at once. Pushing aside the colors, I rose and showered.

Water hot enough to pink my skin seemed to scorch the visions from my head for a moment. I scrubbed the night from face and body. Water beat my hair into obedience.

My body was all hard and manly lines. Cheekbones stood like stones under coarse skin. A short, Irish nose ruined my whole face. Muscles, too big to be girly, rolled under a layer of soft fat. I shaved my legs and arms, my pits. I peeled the skin raw and I smeared lotion over the burning plane. Slick as a seal pup, I looked like a big man, too strong looking to be a real girl.

Memories of the dream scared me. Voices came out of the corners, telling me about the neighbors. The voices told me that Mr. Rothgery, the man on the other side of the fence, was going to kill me. He always made a point of saying hi whenever he saw me, but the voices told me it was all an act. I knew the voices were just voices. They meant nothing. No one wanted me dead, but my head had two parts. There was the part that believed and the part that knew. They fought, working side by side. The noise in my head was brutal and white and sharp.

It was too much. I walked through the kitchen. Tayla sat at the table but said nothing.

Outside, rain streaked the sky. The sidewalks were dark with water. I waited in the wind and the dream walked with me, there and not there, a hand on the back of my neck leading me to the curb. I smoked and paced, and I watched the runners panting in the misty morning.

I closed my eyes and turned away. I looked for the man from my dreams. I looked for him, but he was invisible, watching me, but I couldn't find him.

Tayla brought the car from the garage. I almost didn't get in, but I had school and Tayla was waiting.

"You okay?" Tayla asked.

"Tired."

"Yeah?"

"Nightmares."

Tayla nodded and went back to zooming around cars.

"There was this guy," I said.

"A guy?" she asked.

"A nightmare," I said.

"A nightmare?"

On the other side of the glass, trees rose like twisted priests praying in the gray air. Everything glittered silver for a moment. I thought of my dream. It was both real and unreal. My skin remembered his hands, his lips. I knew about these things. Dreams were sometimes dangerous, especially when they refused to fade in the daylight.

"He was scary," I said.

"Really?"

"Yeah," I said. "We danced."

"Danced?"

"Danced," I said. "But then he…well, you know."

"A sex dream?" Tayla asked.

"Kind of."

"Yuck."

In the Real World

Smokers and stoners hung out in the Shack. The Shack was a shack, sagging clapboard back behind the greenhouses. Years ago, it was a chicken coop. Spaces between the boards let the wind in. Rain dribbled through the ceiling. We kept lawn chairs there. It was a hiding place.

Miss Tris was there with her boyfriend, Tad, passing a small silver pipe back and forth.

Pot smoke floated sweet and thick over me. I didn't smoke pot. It made me weirder than usual. But I had no trouble with anyone else getting high. School sucked enough that the only way some of us could make it through was with a little chemical help.

Miss Tris told us about the club she'd gone to the night before with Tad.

"We danced all night," she said. "I haven't even been to bed yet."

I thought about bed. I thought about the nightmare and wished I could forget for a moment, but I couldn't. Everything turned kind of purple for a moment, as if someone'd punched the air too hard. It flashed then faded. I stood stunned until the bell rang. Tayla kissed me and ran off to choir. I went to physics. This was how the day started, a kiss and a pang of separation, knowing I wouldn't be completely safe again until lunch when Tayla and I sat together scaring all the bullies and popular kids away. I walked through the hall, a target waiting for the bullet, then I saw him standing in the corner down by the choir room, the man from my dream dressed in injured light; deep purple and hazy. I still couldn't see his face, but I knew it was him. He stood there and stared and when I started to walk toward him, he stepped into the crowd and faded away. I spun for a moment, looking for him. He was gone, and I wondered for a moment if I was slipping again. Was this a med thing? Was this the start of another bad patch? I knew I was in trouble, but I didn't completely understand why.

On the Outside

Narrow, gray lockers cut the walls into manageable pieces. Florescent lights refused shadows. Teachers stood in doorways looking for trouble.

I walked among the people. No one looked at me. We all walked with our heads down. They talked among themselves.

Never to me.

People thought they were people. They weren't. They were puppets with strings rising straight into the air. They thought they were free, that their thoughts were their thoughts. No one knew the truth. Whatever pulled the strings was vast and invisible and far from friendly. At best, they were indifferent, too far removed from the real world to care. At worst, they were actively vicious.

I covered my eyes and curled away. I looked for the man from my dreams. Sometimes his face came, a reflection in the window, blurred, purple and featureless. I turned to him, but he went away, and I couldn't find him. He was gone, and I was here with the monsters and the maniacs. I was here, and he was nowhere. I went to class and pretended I was just like everyone else.

Science and Spirit

They made physics the first class of the day and we all gathered in our seats and listened to Mr. Mylenski go on and on about time dilation and the nature of the universe.

"So, you're saying there's no God?" Coy asked.

Coy was a bully, a thundering punk. He pushed himself into the world with all the grace of an ax.

"Coy," Mr. Mylenski said, "this is science." Coy grinned.

"But all knowledge comes from God," Coy said.

Mr. Mylenski closed his eyes for a moment. The boys who followed Coy around chuckled. Even so, some of the folks, most of whom had no room for Coy's foolishness, nodded along. God was a powerful drug. It could turn even the smartest of us into babbling infants.

"That's a question for your priest," Mr. Mylenski said.

"So, there's no room for God in school?" Coy asked.

"Jesus," Mr. Mylenski muttered.

"Exactly," Coy said, smirking.

Some laughter.

"Just stop," I said.

It was supposed to be a thought, a whisper at most, but everyone heard it.

"You have something to say?" Coy asked.

His eyes glittered with cruelty.

"Please," I said.

"Fucking dyke," Coy said.

Everything went quiet. Even the bigots in the room hesitated to cross that line. A special courage filled Coy though. Knowing that most people feared him gave him a vicious confidence.

"Coy," Mr. Mylenski said. "It's time for you to go." They stared at each other, a cockfight. They stared and we all waited to see who would do what. In the end, even there were some things Coy wouldn't do. He grabbed his things and stumped out of the room, muttering.

Mr. Mylenski stood at the head of the class, his face hard and white.

"Anyone else?" he asked.

Silence.

"Okay," he said and started in about split dimensions and infinity. It was interesting, but it was hard to focus on the esoteric thoughts. Shame and fear colored everything. Thoughts spun through my head like shattered glass in a tumbler.

The classroom clock hung on the wall over the whiteboard, right where you'd look when your eyes got tired of staring at the notes on the board. Time stretched. I sat in my seat and watched the second-hand tick. I tried to look away, but I couldn't. My eyes always came back to the clock and the hands barely moved.

My head was heavy and soft. I nodded in and out of focus. Voices seeped through the walls and fell on me like a cold, gentle rain. I watched the shadows of dead people. They moved along the aisles touching people's heads. I wanted to say something, but I didn't. I knew the dead weren't really there. I knew they could do no harm and I had enough grief in my life without adding another episode of talking to the air.

Target

I was neither the biggest kid in school nor the gayest. I was, however, the biggest gay kid and the gayest big kid. Hiding was impossible. Still, all I wanted was to be invisible.

Someone decorated my locker. Someone had taken red nail polish and painted a cross on it. They wrote *God hates dykes too!* I felt sick. I was scared. So I closed my eyes and pretended I didn't see it.

Tayla, though, she saw it. She saw it and she went all warrior dyke, hitting the locker hard enough to break the lock and screaming.

"Your God is a murderer!" She shouted.

Everyone stood around and watched because that's what everyone did. They watched.

"Get your shit," Tayla said.

We walked down the hall.

"You have to stand up for yourself," she said.

I ducked my head and walked a step behind her. That was how I always walked when she was mad. Sometimes, she scared me. Sometimes, she was too much in people's faces. How could I tell her that all I wanted was to disappear? How could I tell her that even when she stood up for me, I felt weak and useless? Tayla didn't want to hear it and she deserved better.

I loved Tayla. I loved dancing. I loved music. But the boys here stared. They stared because I was fat. They stared because they wanted to fuck me. I hated the thought of the men breathing on my tits, the hairs covering my forearms.

Tayla shook her head.

"I just want to dance," I said.

She stopped and turned and I thought that maybe she was going to yell at me. Tayla wanted me to be strong and fierce and all I wanted was a sliver of quiet isolation. Too many people wanted things from me. Tayla wanted courage. Coy wanted control. The school wanted me to go away because just being here made things hard for them.

Tayla softened a little and grabbed my hand.

"Someday," she said, "we'll make it happen someday."

How many, I wondered. How many days would I need to pretend that the eyes didn't bother me? How many days would I need to pretend I could get through this?

Crossing the Line

In English, we talked about poetry and madness. We talked about Ginsberg and his mother. We read *Kaddish* and the sadness nearly killed me.

"Ginsberg was a fag," Coy said.

Mac frowned. Mac didn't tolerate this kind of shit.

"Do you think you're funny?" Mac asked.

"What?" Coy asked. "I was just saying."

"You're always just saying," Mac said.

Mac was a bit of a dandy, prone to paisley shirts and khakis and bow ties. Thin black hair flared around his head in wisps. He was small and thin with dainty-like hands, but his eyes were bright and fierce.

Tayla stood because that's what she did. She stood up to people like Coy.

"Tayla," Mac said.

"The dyke stands," Coy said.

I was sick and scared, but I got out of my chair. I got out of my chair and went to Coy.

Coy was a small boy with big ears and a nose with which he could've caught fish. I stood over him. Tayla came and pressed her hand to my spine, straightening me.

"You need to shut up," I said.

"And the fat one speaks," Coy said.

He smirked and looked around for approval. No one said anything. I punched him in the nose. Bone crunched. Blood flowed. Everyone gasped.

"Jesus," Coy said.

A weird thickness filled the room. No one moved. No one breathed. I was out of my body watching the whole thing from a corner but by the lights. Tayla laughed.

"You fucking hit me," Coy said.

He crawled to his feet, looking for a fight. Tayla pressed her hand to the center of his chest.

"Really?" she asked.

Coy trembled.

"Maybe you need to see the nurse," Mac suggested.

Coy looked around the room. Even his followers refused to back him up.

"Cunts," he said and left.

Everyone stared at me. I hated it when everyone stared at me.

"The dyke strikes back," Tayla said.

She smiled and sat in her chair. I could see the pride in her eyes. I felt sick. Still, it was nice to be in charge for a change.

Episode

Voices and faces bubbled out of the paint on the walls. They were angry faces and their words scraped the flesh from my nerves. I shivered and closed my eyes and hoped no one noticed that today, right now, I was crazier than usual.

Tayla cut her eyes to me off and on. She watched me, and I tried to hide my madness. I guess it didn't work. Halfway through class, Tayla slipped me a note.

You okay?

I closed my eyes.

"Butter?" she whispered.

"No."

"Is it bad?"

I shook my head.

"Butter?"

"I can't."

"Baby," she said. "You're gonna be okay."

"No."

"I'm right here," Tayla said.

She put one hand on my wrist and normally that would have been great, but this time, this time my bones exploded. I imagined little shards punching through my skin and I started sweating and shaking and I was going to puke. I moaned and jerked. Tayla knelt and tried to see my eyes. My head filled with glass and too much light.

"Baby?" Tayla asked.

Slowly, things settled. Light returned. The visions faded. I turned to Tayla and kissed her thin lips. It took a moment, but I smiled, and she smiled. Slowly, trying not to scare me, she gripped my hair.

"I love you," she said.

"Yeah?"

"Absolutely."

"Why?"

She frowned, and I could see the words carving themselves out of her brain, falling onto the back of her tongue before she swallowed them and said, "Impossible not to." And that was how she rescued me.

God Porn

Four girls stood in front of Ms. Wade's class. Ms. Wade taught health. The girls held petitions to their chests. Signs reading *Abstinence Only* sat against the wall. The girls prayed loudly, drawing as much attention as they could.

"God porn," Tayla said.

I wondered if the girls saw their words floating bloody in the thick air. No one paid the girls any mind except Ms. Wade. She stood in her doorway glaring at the girls in their perfect clothes with their perfect hair.

"Look at the tits on Jessica," Tayla said.

Jessica Barber was the dark-headed leader of the group. Her father was the local Mormon Bishop. She wore a silk halter top that played well with her cleavage. I wasn't into the whole good girl look, but boobs were boobs.

"She asked me once what pussy tasted like," Tayla said.

I wasn't sure if that was true. Tayla sometimes liked to say things just to see people's faces.

The girls finished their prayer and spread out, stopping people and asking for signatures. They did this every year. The walls seemed to suck in the bitter air. A shiver ran through me.

"Let's go," Tayla said.

I let her pull me away. I looked back once and noticed the darkness gathering around the smallest girl. I couldn't remember her name, but she was familiar.

"Wait," I said.

Tayla stopped and turned.

"What?"

"I'll be right back," I said.

The air seemed to press on me the closer I got. I stopped just short of them. They all turned to stare at me.

"What?" they asked.

All the courage vanished. I was small again.

"Want to sign the petition?" Jessica asked, sneering a little.

Tayla came and took my hand.

"Not likely," she said, pulling me away.

When we were far enough off, she looked at me.

"What was that?" she asked.

"I thought I saw something," I said.

She schooled her face but stayed quiet. She knew better than to ask questions she didn't want answered.

Lunch

Color drained away except for the bruises blooming around everything. The walls fell soundless to the ground and the ceiling arced into a gray never never land. People faded into shadows and I was there.

He came out of nowhere and pressed himself against my back. Something told me I should be afraid, but I wasn't. I felt nothing. In the real world, in the world where people knew things, I'd have been sick with dread. But this wasn't the real world. This was a world where everything felt like water running over roots.

His bristling chin brushed the back of my neck. When he kissed me between the shoulder blades, my belly caught fire. My thighs tingled and cramped. I tried to touch his cheek, but he pulled away.

"Don't," he said.

"But…"

"I'm here," he said. "I'm here and you're here."

His fingers found my nipples and I yelped. He pumped me full. I was sick with it.

"Hush," he said. "This is a secret."

"What do you want?"

"You."

"No."

"You," he said. "I chose you."

"You chose me?"

"I chose you."

"Why?"

"You can see."

His fingers stroked my chin. I shuddered, trying to knock his hand away.

"Remember," he said. "This is a secret."

Color came back with a crack. Laughter and shouting. Too many people. The smell of cafeteria food scrubbed the last of the vision away. Everyone but Tayla acted as if nothing had happened. They were good at pretending nothing was wrong when everything was wrong.

Miss Tris leaned in.

"I have Ativan," she said.

I shook my head.

"Butter?"

I turned. Tayla stared at me.

"You okay?" she asked.

I swallowed.

"Butter?"

I shook my head. Even here, with the girl I trusted most in the world, I couldn't tell her about a man with no face. That I was afraid; too crazy even for her.

Telling Secrets

Miss Tris sat with me. We had last period off. Tayla had calc and Tad had bio, but Miss Tris signed up for study hall to be with me.

"Tell me about him," she said.

A small pit opened in my belly. I tried not to fall into it.

"Do you believe in angels?" I asked.

She looked out at the cars on the street. A cop slowed for a moment, eyeballing us, before moving on. Technically, we were skipping but as long as we weren't making trouble, no one cared.

"Angels?" Miss Tris asked.

I nodded. She tried hard not to look away.

"Like God's angels?" she asked.

I shrugged.

"There's this guy," I said.

"A guy?"

Her voice was too even, too smooth.

"Never mind," I said.

Her hand took mine. She squeezed my fingers and waited. Waiting was a thing with us. Everyone waited. They waited to see what would come next. They waited to see what to do.

"It's so real," I said.

"But it's not," she said. "Not really."

"It feels real."

"That's all that matters," she said.

Scooting in close, she wrapped an arm around me. It was nice. It was solid.

"Be careful," she said.

I nodded.

"I mean it," she said.

"I know."

"Good."

Kissing my temple, she took me inside. We waited in the cafeteria for Tayla and Tad. When they showed up, Tayla looked questionably at us. So, this was it. Miss Tris was the spy. She didn't say anything though. Nothing about angels. Nothing about weirdness.

"Let's do something," she said instead. "I'm ferociously bored."

Flapping her hands in the air with their bright red nails, she led us through the school, a small queer parade looking for fun.

Water

I danced and Tayla played. Tayla was no dancer. She played a bluesy thing. Soft and slow and sweet. Pounding piano keys turned her into a goddess. She beat the most amazing chords and rhythms. Tayla said that watching me dance gave her ideas. Not the music I danced to but the dancing itself.

I was water. I was a mountain eating the horizon.

Angie flittered around me like a bat looking for food. She danced as if she loved me. Our hearts echoed one another. We knew every muscle and every nerve. Her body was hard and narrow. We breathed into each other's mouths.

But then it ended. Tayla hit the final notes and I found myself on the floor, curled around Angie as if she were the only reason I was alive.

"Jesus," Tayla said.

Absolutely. This was magic. This was redemption. This was divine.

Movie

We smoked too many cigarettes. My gut twisted on itself. My lungs were thick. The walls in Miss Tris's basement were pinkish cinderblock. Couches made a square in the middle of the floor. I was the sober one. I was the one with good judgment. This was not good.

"Let's do something," Miss Tris said.

I shook my head. I wanted to go home. I wanted to sit in a dark room and hide. My nerves quivered.

"Let's go dancing," Miss Tris said. "I need me some loud music."

"You want to get laid," Tad said.

Miss Tris grinned a feral grin.

"That's going to happen anyway," she said. Tad laughed.

"What do you think?" Tayla asked.

She lay on the couch with her head in my lap. My fingers stroked her hair without thought. Just thinking of being in a room with all those people made my fingers flutter.

"I can't drive," I said.

"I can drive," Tad said.

I shook my head. No one here could drive.

"The bus," Miss Tris said.

I shook my head.

"You need to get out," she said.

"I get out," I said.

Everyone laughed at that.

"You'd never leave our room if you had a choice," Tayla said.

She was right. I hated not knowing what was out there. The thought of people nauseated me. The thought of not knowing what people were thinking wrapped my stomach around my spine.

"We have to do something," Miss Tris said. "I'm positively dying."

"How about a movie?" I asked.

It was childish and safe.

"A movie!" Tad said.

He rushed up the stairs.

"Look what you did," Miss Tris said, half joking. "Now I'm going to have to sit through *Fritz the Cat* again."

"Jesus," Tayla said.

Neither of them meant any harm, but I felt small anyway. I felt like I'd ruined everything.

Again.

Surrender

I couldn't refuse him. His hands lifted my breasts and pressed them against my ribs. My spine ached under his lips. I closed my eyes on the lilac smudge covering the word.

My feet tried to walk away, and my knees went loose and weak. What could I do? I was afraid. If I walked away from this, I'd pay. He would pound me into the ground. All I could do was wait for it to be over.

He reached around and dropped my jeans. He bent me over the table and slid into me, pounding and swelling until I could barely stand. Everything went pale then dark. There was no telling what would happen if I fell. I felt him come and pulled free.

His hands slid from my shoulders to my hips and released me. Opening my eyes, I waited for him to say something, but my body knew he was gone. I felt sick and dizzy and sore.

Pulling my pants up, I rushed to the bathroom and puked. I puked until I thought I might pass out. Cramps knotted my belly. My body remembered the feel of him inside of me. It was over. For now.

Insomnia

Sun rise. Jays screamed in the rhodies and roses. He came, an indigo shadow, a dream following me. When he touched me, I shivered.

He asked if I loved him. I didn't know what to say. I lit a cigarette. He stroked my face. My eyes watered. Heat crackled along my jaw and cheekbones.

"What is this?" I asked.

"I chose you," he said.

I shook my head.

"You're beautiful," he said.

I turned away.

"What are you?" I asked.

"A dream," he said. "A hope."

"What does that mean?"

"Call me Gid," he said.

The light turned thick, the color of a fresh bruise, smooth as a marble floor. Mt. Hood stood like a broken tooth. He said nothing. I told myself this was a dream but it was more than a dream. It was real. It was frightening. I hated it.

Suddenly, music. Miles Davis.

"Come," he said. He took my hand. I didn't remember reaching for him, but he lifted me to my feet and I lay my head on his chest's broad plane. Music circled us. His face was a smudge of ash.

Wind lifted us into an empty, lilac sky. I wanted to scream, but he held me too tight. I couldn't breathe. Flying was terrifying. I wanted to puke. I wanted to put my feet on the ground.

Suddenly, the world stopped spinning and we stood in a room with no walls.

"This is all yours," he said.

"There's nothing here," I said.

"Not yet."

His hands stroked my spine.

"All you have to do is love me," he said.

Light came from the hall. Gid disappeared. Tayla stood there staring at me.

What do I do now? I thought. *This is not good.*

Love and Madness

Our bed was old. Knots of stuffing kneaded my spine. Springs tried to push through, to stab me in the ribs. Tayla lay next to me reading *The Dead Man Poems*.

"There's this guy," I said. "He's following me around."

Tayla's eyes got wide. She put her hand on my wrist. "What's going on?"

"There's this guy," I said.

I petered out for a second. Things got strange and thin. Images fluttered like leaves through my mind. A faceless man. Hands wrapped around my waist. A dick, huge and fierce, stabbing into my belly. I wanted to punch him. I wanted him to get the hell away and let me go back to my crazy but comfortable life.

"Butter?" Tayla said.

"A dream," I said.

Tayla got this look on her face. I knew this look. This was the look she got when she was starting to think that maybe I was losing it. I'd seen it before. Too many times. It was a closed, hard look. I hated it.

"I'm fine," I said.

"Really?" she asked.

I shrugged.

"It's a dream."

Doubt soured things for a moment, but then she kissed me.

"What do you need?"

"I don't know," I said.

And that was it. She kissed me and smiled. There were things between us, time and history, scars and scares. Something was coming but there was nothing we could do about it, so I pretended it didn't matter.

Lost Meaning

I danced. Alone. I danced in the darkness of my room. My body lost meaning when I moved like this. The edges blurred. I was in the world but not of it. I floated over everything. Music stroked my bones and I was not a fat, teenaged lesbian. I was not a crazy girl. No one hated me. I scared no one. I was more than a soft thing in a hard world. I was divine.

I turned and there he was, wrapped in violets.

"Shit," I said.

"Beautiful," he said.

I shuddered.

He came and lifted me. My hips turned to wings and I rose into a sky suddenly filled the color of dawn. He spun me and I fell forever.

"I'm right here," he said and I hit the floor, hard. Pain flashed in my back. When I opened my eyes, I was alone but then Tayla was there.

"Butter," she said from the door.

"I'm okay," I said.

"Yeah?"

"Yeah."

It took a moment but then she turned and left. I was alone but not alone. He stood in the corner, watching.

"You can't tell her," he said.

"Why?"

Nothing. Silence.

"What do you want?" I asked.

More silence. The smell of lilacs and lavender. I didn't know what was happening. All I knew was that it was only beginning. I knew that the shit was getting thick and it pissed me off.

Someday

Queertopia was the last table in the last row in the cafeteria, right next to the Ag hall. The Shack was one door and a short walk away. Next to us, the stoners sat in Stonerville. They didn't bother us. Being on the edges of everything gave us both a kind of mutual respect if not friendship.

We talked about dancing.

"There's Haven," Tad said.

I shook my head.

"Too many people," I said.

"There's The Hole," Tayla said.

The Hole was a jazz spot.

"No one dances at The Hole," Tad said.

"What's with you people and dancing?" Tayla asked. "Is that all you do?"

"Party and play," Miss Tris shouted.

Laughter rolled through the room. For a moment we thought it was us but then we saw Coy up-front dancing around with a mop between his legs, moaning like a porn star. People loved that shit.

"Jesus," I said.

We shook our heads.

"Someday," Tad said. "Someone's going to hurt that boy."

"Someday," Tayla said, looking fierce.

I nodded. Someday. We all waited for someday.

Poverty

Dinner was one egg, a piece of toast made from hard bread. Beans and rice. I wasn't hungry, but I pretended I was. Gid sat with us at the table.

"It's poisoned," he said.

I salted everything into submission. Tayla watched me, her face sad.

"I get paid this week," Tayla said.

I nodded.

"I'm doing the best I can," she said.

I pushed the food around, afraid to eat, ashamed of my fear. Gid pushed his foot into my crotch and I twitched.

"Are you shy?" he asked, purple laughter in his throat.

I shook my head.

"This," he said, "is life."

"No."

Tayla watched me with narrow eyes.

"I'm okay," I said.

"Are you?" she asked.

"It's nothing," I said.

Something hard passed through her face.

"I'll never leave you," Gid said.

I swallowed. I tried to look at Tayla. I wanted her to see me get through this. I couldn't, and she didn't.

"Lovely," she said.

"See," Gid said.

Tayla put her plate in the sink, food and all. Something heavy weighed on her.

"I'm sorry," I said.

She nodded and went to the living room and lay on the couch. I followed and stopped.

There were no words. There were no excuses or explanations, only space and loneliness.

Unconditional

I couldn't make my legs work. The lights drilled directly into my skull. Cars screamed loud and dangerous on the street outside. What was I supposed to do? I closed my eyes.

Gid came and sat with me, dressed in king's robes made of light and lilies. He said nothing. Even here, his face was invisible behind a livid smudge. I wanted to touch him. I had so many questions, but my tongue was too swollen to speak. He just stared at me and shook his head.

He rose and stood in the corner and for some reason I cried. Tears burned my cheeks. I couldn't breathe. I felt sick.

The room spun. Gid ran his finger along my spine. My bones shuddered. I puked.

"You're killing yourself," he said.

I lie on the floor and felt his breath on my neck. How am I going to get out of this? I closed my eyes. Somehow, I knew when he left. I knew when I was alone. But only for a moment. Tayla shook me.

"Jesus," she said. "Are you okay?"

I opened my eyes. Vomit crusted my chest and belly. It spread in a chunky pool over the carpet.

"Butter," she said.

Her voice was tight with worry and anger. Nothing was simple with Tayla.

"You need a shower," she said.

I was too weak to move. Tayla lifted me.

"Come on," she said.

The bathroom's naked bulb blinded me. I fell again.

"Shit," Tayla said.

I wanted to say something but how do you tell someone about a dream that walks in the real world? Gid was right. I was dying.

Voices and Visions

Night. Everything was the color of plums. No stars. No moon. No light but for the fire at the end of my cigarette. Rain, a simple mist, and mountainous winds.

Three days without sleep. Voices told me I was dying, that it would be better, less painful, if I did it myself. Dark figures reached for me like the ghosts of so many forgotten memories.

I shuddered and tried not to cry. Maybe the voices were right. Maybe dying would be easier. At least then, I'd rest. But I couldn't. Tayla would never forgive me. She'd crumble to dust.

Trees at the edge of the yard held their naked hands to the sky, wooded priests singing a silent mass. A cat slinked like a thief along the fence. This early in the morning everything seemed thick and shady. The world seemed to wait for something. Tension held everything together, just barely.

I waited. I waited and smoked, and I listened to the robins screaming up the day. Soon the sun would rise, and I'd see the world, hard and edgy and maybe I'd split myself open.

My throat felt gritty and sour. If this was it, if I were to die right now, I knew I'd make more pain than I ended, but did it matter? Would anyone notice I was gone?

Sour

The world was quiet, and I curled up on the couch. I must have slept. When I opened my eyes, Gid sat with me, bruising the light with his massive hands. There was no escape.

"Go away."

"You need to wake up," he said.

"No."

"I'm not going to stop just because you don't like it."

"I don't want you here."

He stared at me with his invisible eyes. A slimy sweat broke out along my ribs. He was gone but he'd be back. He ruined everything. He soured the very air I breathed.

Answered Questions

Tayla sat in the living room and stared at the television. Her eyes drooped and blinked. She looked too tired. She worked long hours. She went to school and she giggled. She did her homework and stumbled through the days as best she could. We lived hand to mouth.

"It won't last forever," she used to say.

She was wrong. Her mom died and mine sent me away. This was how things stood, hard and cold and barely livable.

"Hey," I said.

She looked up. Dark circles made her old. My stomach wrapped itself around my spine.

"What's wrong?" she asked.

I looked out the window. A bat cut the dusk to ribbons. I turned away.

"Butter?"

I swallowed. Voices whispered in the walls. They told me she would hate me for this.

"Nothing," I said.

I walked into the kitchen. There was a whole drawer of knives there. The kitchen was dangerous. I could die there. Tayla came and touched me. Her hand was cold and heavy.

"What's up?" she asked.

"Do you believe in God?" I asked.

"Jesus."

I swallowed.

"Hell scares me," I said.

Tayla laughed.

"Hell's for Baptists," she said. "There's no room in Hell for dykes like us."

It was a joke. Kind of. I tried to smile, but I was too scared. Tayla was too tired. She went back to the couch and lay down. I watched her sleep for a long time wondering if her dreams scared her as much as mine scared me.

A Thing

Homecoming. I didn't want to go. Tayla hated the very thought. But Miss Tris talked us into it.

"It's a Thing," she said. "Dressing up. Acting all grown up," Tayla snorted.

"Grown-ups don't do this shit," she said.

"Exactly," Miss Tris said. "It's a Thing. A high school Thing."

She bought the tickets. She tried to talk us into dresses but neither Tayla nor I went for that. Tayla wore a suit she got from Goodwill, gray linen, shiny in spots but not bad. She wore a purple shirt under it.

I wore jeans and a plaid shirt, Doc Martins. Miss Tris came to the door and made a face.

"You look like a couple of dykes," she said.

"We are a couple of dykes," Tayla said.

For a moment, Miss Tris looked like she was going to argue with us but Tad squeezed her hand and she swallowed whatever fight she had and nodded. Tad winked when I looked at him and I grinned. Maybe this wasn't going to be too bad.

Outside, night fell bit by bit. A tattered cloak of clouds shot through with the reds and purples of blood and bruises covered the sky. Things were dry. Trees stood gnarled and dark along the streets.

Miss Tris drove her dad's Mustang. The car was old but nice, bright red and shiny. I knew nothing of these things, but it was a sweet ride.

"It's a classic," Miss Tris said. "Dad and I rebuilt it ourselves."

An image of Miss Tris in greasy overalls, her perfectly painted nails twisting wrenches and lifting oily metal things out from under the hood played through my imagination. Laughter bubbled out of my chest.

"What?" Miss Tris asked.

"Just thinking of you with tools," I said.

"She's great with tools," Tad said.

That made Tayla laugh.

"Perverts," Miss Tris said, but she grinned too.

Cars filled the parking lot. Everyone wore suits and pretty, pretty dresses. Dread chilled the moment. Fun time was over. Something bad was about to happen.

"You coming?" Miss Tris asked when I hesitated.

I nodded.

"You okay?" Tad asked.

I shrugged. Tayla squeezed my hand. A couple folks stopped to stare. Being small town queers, we were used to a certain amount of staring. We walked boldly to the door. Miss Tris had our tickets out. Mr. Skarey looked at us, all sad eyes and stern.

"I'm sorry," he said.

We stopped cold.

"There's a dress code," he said.

People gathered and snickered.

"What?" Tayla asked, dangerously.

I closed my eyes.

"You have to dress the part," Mr. Skarey said. "Appropriately."

"What's wrong with our clothes?" Miss Tris asked.

"Michael," he said.

"Tris," Miss Tris hissed.

Mr. Skarey swallowed. He saw the fight coming and there was nothing he could do.

"There are rules," he said, weakly.

"Fuck your rules," Tayla snarled.

I backed away. People were really staring now. They gathered for the drama.

"I can't let you in," Mr. Skarey said.

"We have tickets," Tad said.

"Sorry," he said. "That was a mistake." Tension hung thick. I felt sick.

"I can't," I said.

I turned to go but Tayla wouldn't let go of my hand. She was forcing me to stay.

"Please," I said.

"No," Tayla said.

We stood there, three angry queers and me. Tad moved close and took my free hand. Behind us a group of Goth girls giggled, all torn black stockings and leather miniskirts. They smelled of weed and Schnapps.

"This is shit," Tayla said.

"You need to go," Mr. Skarey said.

For a long time, nothing happened. I thought maybe Tayla was going to throw a punch. That would've made it perfect. But she turned slowly and dragged me away.

"Told you this was a bad fucking idea," she said.

Miss Tris stammered, pale under her makeup.

"Just take us home," Tayla said.

We loaded into the Mustang.

"A Thing," Tayla said. "Fucking beautiful."

Promise

Gid stood in the corner solid and beautiful. Amethyst darkness masked his face. I wanted to run away. I wanted nothing to do with him. But Gid never asked me what I wanted. He took me when he wanted me. He wrote his name on my nerves. He lifted me from the bed. Tayla rolled over and whispered something I couldn't understand. All I wanted was to lie with her. All I wanted was to sleep without dreams or memories.

But no. He lifted me. He opened the skin of my palm and licked the skin.

"No," I said.

He made a circle on my forehead with his finger.

"This," he said, "is a promise."

"This," he said, "makes you mine."

It brought a kind of euphoria. Different from dancing. Different from anything in the world but real and toxic as heroin. The rush of attention turned me soft. I waited. I looked for his face.

"Why are you doing this?" I asked.

He laughed.

"Am I going to Hell?" I asked. "I've done nothing wrong."

"People like you need people like me," he said.

His finger wrote something in the center of my chest.

"People like me?"

"I exist because of you," he said. "You exist because of me."

"This is nuts."

He kissed my chin.

"Yes."

He walked away. The high ended. I jerked awake and stared at the ceiling. A spider made its way among the cracks and creases. Voices and faces leered and screamed.

People like me? I asked myself.

Tayla rolled over and looked at me.
"You okay?" she asked.
I flinched a little. Not sure why.
"Yeah," I lied. "Perfect."

Pretty Words

"Do you love me?" Tayla frowned.
"Of course, I love you." I shook my head.
"Why?"
Tayla laughed.
"Impossible not to," she said.

Pretty words. All glass and gold. I floated away and painted suicidal fantasies on the walls of my skull. If I could live forever, I'd love everyone, but I wouldn't, and I didn't. All I knew was that Tayla, the girl holding my hand, knew the way home. She held my hand and rubbed the tendons between the bones.

"Come on," she said. "Just breathe."

It was the sound of her voice that saved me. It was the sound of her voice that made it okay to open my eyes.

Delusions

I was too cold. White air sucked the wind from my lungs. I shivered, and I hurt. Gid came and pushed his hand into my chest. My ribs shattered in violet shards. My guts turned to water. I felt as if I'd shit myself. Gid spun me in tight circles.

"All of this is yours," he said. "Just take it."

My legs cramped. My hands hurt. Blood poured from my palms, the arches of my feet. He pressed his dick against my ass.

"Stop," I said.

My voice was weak and thin. The words rose like fog in a wind, breaking apart. He reached around and shoved a finger into me. Ice cut through my thighs. I screamed. I screamed and screamed.

"This is your world," he said. "This is all you have."

Somehow, I woke. A tree limb tapped on the glass. I felt for Tayla but she wasn't there. I was too scared to sleep. I was too scared to get up. Everything hurt. Everything pressed on me. All I could do was cry and wait. Tayla came out of the bathroom.

"Hey," she said. "What's wrong?"

She lifted my face to look at her. All I could do was babble.

"It's okay," she said.

She had no idea.

"Butter," Tayla said. "I'm right here."

Her warm hands saved me. When she kissed me, my chest opened. My heart beat.

"I'm dying," I said.

She shook her head.

"No," she said. "It only feels like it."

A Dream in Daylight

Coy was small and mean. His head was too big for his body. Kinky black hair lay like a mat of steel wool. Arrogance swelled his narrow chest. People pissed him off. Not that he'd had a good life. Scars on his thighs and back told a secret history. Not that he ever said anything.

His eyes, green as old money, took everything in but gave nothing back. He danced from group to group. No one really liked him. Even the people with whom he spent all his school time didn't hang with him in the evenings or weekends. Under the hallway lights at school, he was pale as a dream in daylight.

Coy sold pills and powders out of his locker and car between classes, in the morning, at lunch. Dope made him powerful. Watery-eyed stoners followed him around. They piled cash in Coy's pocket.

Coy set the stoners after us. He paid them to jump Miss Tris in the hall. To them, it was just a gag, but when Miss Tris lay on the hallway floor, bleeding and hurt, Tad went a little nuts. He chased people through the halls. Folks screamed. Some of them laughed. They pointed and cheered him on. Tad cornered one boy in the gym and wailed the hell out of him with a broomstick. The boy ended up in the ER with broken ribs, bruises, and stitches; the cops came for Tad. They gave him forty hours of community service.

"Totally worth it," Tad said. "I just wish it was Coy."

Room

A creek ran on the edge of town. Brown water whirled around fallen trees and stones. It swirled around the legs of a small bridge on a small road. Ferns and moss turned the banks green.

Oak and chestnut arced over everything.

I was cold and wet and the wind coming from the mountains cut the bones in my neck and arms.

I stood on the bridge and I stared at the water, and in my head I saw it flowing slowly to the river and the river flowed to the ocean. The ocean washed the world and the world turned. I thought, maybe, if I were to jump in here, I would wash up on a distant shore, away from the eyes and words constantly pushing against me. If I were to jump now, I would be part of the real world. I would live forever.

At home, Tayla grabbed me.

"Where have you been?" she asked, her voice both shivering and sharp.

"I went for a walk," I said.

"Jesus," she said.

"I know how to take of myself," I said.

"I was scared."

I went to our room. I went to bed. I dreamed of disappearing. I dreamed of being a memory. I dreamed of no one bothering me. Right now, there were too many people, too many demands. Right now, there was no room left for me.

Return

    I neither slept nor woke. It was not a dream, but it was. Tayla's ass pressed hot against my hip. Mattress springs jabbed me in the kidneys. My lungs struggled. I couldn't move. Something heavy pressed me into the earth. Bones turned to stone. Blood to water. Flesh to mud. I faded, but then Gid called my name. I rose, Lazarus-like.

    He walked with me. Heat rolled from him in bright waves like a lily opening. Everything rose in angles. Mountains ate at the horizon, purple and sharp as broken teeth. The sky arced over us, endless and smooth as marble.

    "This is beautiful," I said.

    He reached out to me. My flesh crawled.

    "Don't do that," he said.

    He sounded almost sad. The edges of his body frayed a little. A strange sympathy stirred through me. But then his fingers pressed against my throat. White fire flared. I would've screamed had I been able.

    "I'm sorry," he said. "This is needed." Everything quivered.

    "Look," he said.

    I opened my eyes.

    "This is what there is," he said.

    The ground rose around me, grinding and crushing. Darkness. I was a stain, all tears and shit. All I had left was a skeletal hope that this would end somehow, that the sun would rise and rescue me.

Questions

Water dribbled through a space in the Shack's ceiling. The air was dim and smoky. Miss Tris sat in a lawn chair, stoned, staring at the wavering flags from our cigarettes.

"Do you believe in God?" I asked.

She looked at me with soft, fuzzy eyes. Today, orange light spiked around her.

"What do you mean?" she asked.

"Do you think God is real?" I asked.

A smile spread in her gentle face. Her eyes blinked slowly while she thought.

"Not sure," she said.

Her hands reached for something only she could see.

"Why do you ask?" she asked.

"I met a guy," I said.

That got her focused for a moment.

"A guy?"

I nodded.

"A guy guy?"

Another nod.

"That complicates things."

A hint of disapproval echoed in her mouth.

"It's not love," I said. "He comes when he comes."

"Physical though?" she asked.

"Not sure," I said.

Confusion in her face. Slowly, the words tumbled into the room. They gathered in a huge pile of crazy. It was all so ridiculous and sad and real. It was solid and scary.

"I think maybe he's a god," I said.

She laughed.

"What gave you that idea?" he said.

"I don't know," I said.

She put her hand on my knee.

"It's just a thing," she said. "It'll pass."

I nodded. Maybe. Maybe not. Maybe this was what my life was now. Fear. Shame. Pain.

Show

Folks came through the door, talking and shuffling around the seats with their programs and social skills. I watched them through a crack in the curtain. They mixed and talked. Voices turned to white noise. Nerves twanged through my chest. I felt sick. I felt high. I shivered and stretched in the wings. Angie rubbed the muscles along my spine.

"We're going to fly," she said.

I always got this way before a show. I wanted to run and I wanted to tear my own heart out. Sweat turned my palms slick.

When the lights changed, Angie and I took to the stage. We stood and waited and music ramped up out of nothing. Hard rhythms rattled ribs and the floors. Movement. A moment of absolute terror before my body took over and made everything magic. The world dropped away. I was no longer the fat, manly girl. I was light and heat. Angie was a ball of lightning.

But then, he was there. He stood in the wings, watching, wrapped in twilight. I nearly fell. I nearly froze, but I didn't. I sucked in hot air and spun away. Time turned to water. Things got real simple. Move. Lift and spin. This was love. This was power. This was strength. This would save me from everything.

More Trouble

Coy came looking for trouble. He came looking for a fight. I tried to ignore him. I tried to pretend he wasn't there. But he was there. He stood in my way. He put a hand in the middle of my chest. His buddies snickered.

"Don't touch me," I said.

"Don't touch me," Coy mocked. "You're a fat one," he said.

I was. I was fat. Thick thighs held broad hips. Hands like oars hung from heavy arms. I was strong but soft. A target. People talked about me, mostly behind my back. Coy, though, he wanted to see my face when he said it. He wanted to see me cry.

I tried to step around him but he slid into my way again. He pushed his narrow chest into me, his face just inches from my face.

"You smell like pussy," he said. "Maybe if you shaved that beard."

"Leave me alone," I said.

Still, I touched my chin. Was that roughness whiskers? Jesus.

Coy's grin said he saw it and I hated that he saw it.

"Why would I do that?" he asked.

His hand came to my face and I backed away.

"You need to go," I said.

He offered me twenty bucks for a blowjob. He smelled of weed and cigarettes. He smelled of hatred and violence. His eyes bugged from their sockets, froggish and dull. He raised his hand and I grabbed it. I twisted and shoved, and he fell. He got up and came after me. I swung. Blood flew and flowed. He dropped to the floor.

"Jesus," he said. "Fuck. You broke my nose."

His face was a mess in his hands. For a moment, I felt badly for him. But then he stood and started for me. Violence gathered in his fists and face. I swung. He screamed and fell again. I almost bashed him with my foot, but Gid came. He stood, staring, one hand up.

"Stop," he said.

I didn't want to stop. My hands shook ,and I felt sick and if I stopped now, Coy might get up again. I couldn't have him getting up again.

Tayla came. She stopped and stared. She took everything in. Light turned to individual dusty grains. I wanted to puke. I wanted to run. There was nowhere to go. Gid stayed in his corner, his face filled with darkness.

"Stop," he said.

Tayla stopped and took in the scene. Before moving, she told me to breathe.

"Time to go," Tayla said and steered me down the hall.

Fear and anger turned my skin to thin paper. I didn't know how I did what I did. I collapsed.

"This is shit," Tayla said.

"What else was I supposed to do?" I asked.

"Walk away," she said.

I shook my head. How did you walk away when there was nowhere to go?

Consequences

Pastel landscapes hung in perfect rows on the walls. I sat there and stared out the window at a murder of crows cutting through the sky. I sat there and wondered what was going to happen to me.

"Butter," Mr. Skarey said. "You could have killed that boy."

"I thought about that."

A little fear crossed through his eyes. I felt bad.

"What're we going to do about this?" he asked.

I shook my head.

"Butter…"

"He called me a dyke," I said.

Mr. Skarey shook his head.

"I'm sorry," I said.

He put his fingertips together and frowned.

"What am I supposed to do?" he asked.

Thoughts of suicide floated through my mind. Voices told me how worthless things were. They told me that it be so much better if I were dead.

Gid's voice seeped into my head, like old blood.

"They hate you," he said.

I closed my eyes.

"They're going to kill you," he said.

For a moment, it felt like he was in the room with us, but no one saw him.

"You need to run," he said.

This was how it happened. I knew I needed help but if I told anyone about him, they'd lock me up again and I couldn't stand the thought of that. Psych wards were all thick walls and windows that wouldn't open and people who spent too much time talking to ghosts.

"I love you," he said.

Was this love? I didn't know. All I knew was that it tasted of blood and ash. It cut through me like a glass blade.

Time Out

Even at sunset, Hagg Lake was green. Green pines and firs bristled from ridges. Algae stained the water. Red and yellow light stood out hard behind the mountains. Tayla and I shared a bottle of wine.

"You did the right thing," she said.

"I was so scared," I said.

Tayla smiled.

"People are going to talk about this forever," she said.

Tayla needed the world to see her. All I wanted was a corner to hide in. The thought of people talking about this made me more than a little sick.

"Can you make it stop?" I asked.

Tayla laughed.

"This is a good thing," she said. "You're a sexy dyke goddess."

I trembled. Not a goddess. A sacrifice maybe, a goat on the altar.

Spells in the Corner

The music was enormous, filled with ragged bones. It was dark and dangerous. Cigarettes painted the room gray and blue. Old men and scrawny women sat at the bar guarding their drinks, smoking too much, talking about work and religion. Everything smelled of kitchen grease.

Tayla wove spells in the corner. She played with her eyes closed. She was there and not there at the same time. I could almost see her ghost hanging in the rafters watching the whole thing. Her body knew the secrets she was trying to tell. She didn't need to listen anymore to the music her hands made.

People bobbed and nodded at the tables, letting the notes rock them like children waiting for sleep. Tayla cut through them with a blue and silver wind.

She got me in by telling the door guy that I was her sound person, which was dumb because there were no mics or speakers. Tayla didn't need tech to capture folks.

I sat at the bar smoking a cigarette, mesmerized. A thin man with a pot belly over narrow hips eased up to me. He looked like a four-legged spider. I wanted nothing to do with him. Spiky black hair covered his head. He smelled of cigarettes and beer and bad meat.

"Can I buy you a drink?" he asked.

I shook my head.

"One drink," he said.

He pushed his face close to me.

"That's my girlfriend," I said, pointing to Tayla.

"Girlfriend?"

"Girlfriend."

"Jesus."

He walked away. That was how it always ended. Disgust and judgment.

Missionaries

Two boys came around the corner. They wore black suits and carried black bibles. I watched them from the window. They walked shoulder to shoulder, upright and proper. They were pretty enough to be a couple, but they probably weren't.

Bone-colored light hung from them in long streamers. Voices told me to hide. They told me these boys were thieves coming to steal my soul. They were celestial salesmen selling false hope. I watched them like a mouse watching an owl. But then it came to me.

"Shit," I said.

Tayla looked up from the floor.

"What?"

"Mormons."

Tad opened his eyes, his head in Miss Tris's lap.

"Jesus," he said.

"Get away from the window," Tayla snapped.

I couldn't though. If the Mormons were coming here, I wanted to see them.

"Butter," Tayla cried.

It was too late. The boys stopped in front of our place and looked around. They started across the yard.

"Here they come," I said, strangely indifferent.

Tayla got up.

"Fuck," she said.

The missionaries knocked. Something electric flashed through me. I hated it when people knocked on our door. Not even knowing it was going to happen helped.

"Hush," Tayla said.

Miss Tris shot off the couch and into the kitchen.

"Wait," she called.

"What're you doing?" Tayla asked.

Silence. We looked at Tad. He shrugged.

"Just wait," he said. "It's hilarious."

"Okay," Miss Tris called from the kitchen. "Let them in."

"What? No!"

Tayla had no love for Christians of any stripe and Mormons prickled especially hard for some reason.

"Baptizing the dead!" she always said, like it was the most horrible thing ever.

"And forever families," I reminded her.

She clenched her teeth and grunted.

"Exactly," she'd growl.

Tayla's family was not a family anyone would want to be stuck with forever.

Back in the living room, Tad went to the door. I blocked him.

"Trust me," he said.

Looking back and forth from Tad to Tayla and across the room to the kitchen. I looked to Tayla again. She shrugged. I sucked in a deep breath, as if the missionaries were there to cut out my heart. They knocked again.

"Okay," I said and opened the door.

Bits of the world shot at me like jagged glass. I winced. The Mormons pretended not to see.

"Inda Butterfly?" the tall one asked.

His face was too smooth. All the parts fit together too well. He looked like a news guy. I didn't like him.

"Ma'am?" he asked.

I nodded.

"We're looking for Inda Butterfly," he said.

Tad and Tayla came to the door. The missionaries stepped back.

"Can I help you?" Tad asked.

Tad's face was hard and pointed. His voice crackled a little.

"Bishop Barber sent us," the smaller boy said.

He looked a little like a cat, wide-eyed, wary but trying to be indifferent.

"Bishop Barber?" I asked.

"Why?" Tad asked.

Fear mixed with courage changed the colors around the boys to a dark yellow, shot through with greasy green. The tall one swallowed and the small one held out a hand.

"I'm Paul," he said.

We stared at him.

"We want none of it," Tayla said.

Tad put a hand on Tayla's shoulder. She glared at him.

"Wait," Tad said.

"Bishop Barber," the tall boy said, "thought you might want a little spiritual guidance."

"Guidance?" I asked.

"Help," Paul said.

Tayla growled. I wanted to close the door but Tad stopped me.

"We thought you might like to hear about Our Heavenly Father."

That was when things turned odd. Miss Tris came flying out of the kitchen wrapped in the curtains and nothing else. Her dick and tits wagged and bounced. The Mormons gasped and froze. They looked from me to Tad, from Tayla to Miss Tris.

"Evening boys!" Miss Tris cried.

She was bright and lovely and divine. The Mormons paled. The colors around them burned yellow and green. Something in me snapped. Laughter filled the room.

"Kisses!" Miss Tris cried, rushing forward.

The Mormons stumbled and turned. They didn't run, not quite, but they hurried. Tayla lay on the floor gasping and choking with laughter.

"Told you," Tad said.

He did. He told us and he delivered. This was a forever story.

Doorway

It happened fast and it lasted forever. Tayla walked with me through the parking lot. Sunlight burned through thin clouds. Budding leaves sang in the trees. A raven told lies in the sky. Because I was always scared, and I always watched everyone all of the time, I saw Coy and I assumed the woman with him was his mother because they wore the same face except for the bruises and the tape over the ridge of his nose. I stopped and then Tayla stopped. She looked at me and then she looked at the door.

"Shit," she said.

Time got thick and the day got heavy. I could barely move. Something was going to happen. I wanted it to just be a normal day. I wanted it to be one of those days that no one talked to me. I wasn't ready for name-calling and the bullying. Tayla grabbed my hand and pulled. I couldn't move.

"Come on," she said.

"No."

"Butter," she said. "We have to do this."

I shook my head. I wasn't ready. I didn't want to.

"Come on," Tayla said. "What can they do?"

Mr. Skarey came and stood with them and my gut went hollow.

"This should be good," Tayla said.

She half-dragged me to the door. She squared off with Coy and his mother. Mr. Skarey looked like he'd licked a slug.

"We have to talk," he said.

"No," Tayla said.

Mr. Skarey blinked.

"We're not doing this," Tayla said.

Something sharp and hard seemed to press through the palms of my hands. I rubbed them with my fingertips.

"I don't think you understand," Mr. Skarey said.

"I understand," Tayla said. "Not going to happen."

Coy sneered. His mother's face looked like a stewed tomato.

"Young lady," Mrs. Henderson said.

"Not talking to you," Tayla snapped.

"I'm talking to you," Mrs. Henderson snapped back.

The two of them stared at each other. Mrs. Henderson was all lines and angles and righteousness. Tayla was simply defiance and rage.

"Are you going to call the cops?" Tayla asked.

"I don't think we need to do that," Mr. Skarey said.

"Didn't think so."

Tayla dragged me through the door into the school. Eyes and grins floated out of the walls. The colors here were orange and yellow, floating and waving like banners.

"Did you have to do that?" I asked.

I would've been just as happy at home.

"Seven more months," Tayla said. "Seven more months and we're out of here. They're not taking that away from us."

Tayla's need for a fight, her need to be right, was one of my least favorite things.

Fighting's easy when you have nothing to lose. Tayla didn't understand how dangerous things were. She didn't understand that she was the only thing keeping me here. She didn't understand that mouthy women seldom lived long in a world of angry men.

Visions

People talked. They talked about me. Their faces stretched into bony masks. I sat against the hallway wall. Colors eddied like smoke and confetti. Things sparkled and shivered. I shivered and waited. I waited for everything to go away.

Sparkles spun in the watery light. No one saw what I saw. There were monsters here. Monsters and angels. Demons and dragons. My stomach turned and a bell rang. People faded into classrooms and walls. I was alone but not alone.

Suicide fantasies invaded me, slimy green and pus yellow. Blood and sinew. Sadness and shame. Another bell. The walls leaned over me, threatening to eat me alive. I shrunk into my spine and tried to find somewhere safe. But nowhere was safe. Nowhere.

I sucked air through my teeth. I shivered and cried. I floated somewhere where the light was heavier than me. But then the faces and the voices fell away. Slowly, I came back to myself. I was alone again. I went to the Shack and lit a cigarette.

This was how my life worked: voices, visions and habits that were going to kill me someday.

PE

I watched the game without watching the game. Whistles and shouts echoed from the walls, mixing into waves of static. Basketball held no interest for me. I had to take PE but they couldn't make me play. So I sat in the bleachers with Miss Tris. She too had to take the class, but they wouldn't let her in the locker rooms. People didn't like the idea of a girl like her sharing showers with their kids.

"Pretty," Miss Tris said.

Tad played on the court with the rest of the folks. Sweat shined on his dark skin. He moved with a wild kind of grace. Watching him was like watching a bird fly. Even then, Tad couldn't hold my attention. Things rumbled through my head. Voices whispered secrets. Faces formed and fractured in the walls. Everything was red and black.

Miss Tris took my hand and looked at me.

"Can I help?" she asked.

I shook my head.

"I'm right here," she said.

My heart beat. My head buzzed. Miss Tris held my hand, but her eyes wandered onto the court again. I looked too. Jessica Barber launched a shot from the three-point line. Her tits rose and fell like a shelf shifting. It was glorious and beautiful. It was enough to make me forget for a moment that my life sucked.

Alone But Then Not

    I danced with the light. Silver angels and blue demons twirled around me. Count Basie caressed my bones and I stretched my body on the carpeted floor. Bass rattled through my ribs, making it hard to breathe, making my heart fall out of rhythm. I was all muscle and tendon, far more butch than femme.
    I spun and reached. I jumped and flew, if only for a moment. Gravity pulled me down and I rolled, burning my shoulders and hips on the floor. Light flew through the windows, golden and speckled with dust. Nothing mattered but the music and the movement.
    Sweat soaked my cleavage and ran in thin streams into my eyes. When I couldn't move anymore, I lay on the floor and stared at the textured ceiling. I don't know how long I stayed there. Awhile. I lay there and everything fell away.
    Gid lay on the couch staring at me. There and not there. A bruise rapidly fading. He said nothing. A weird rage lit in my head. All I could see was a whiteness that threatened to blind me. Just having him there poisoned everything.
    "Beautiful," he said. "Divine."
    He was wrong. Nothing about me was divine. I was young and fat. I was the girl looking out at a world that refused to look back. People either hated me or ignored me.
    "Someday," Gid said. "Someday you'll jump and never come down."
    What did that mean? I mean, gravity always won. No matter what you did, you always ended up on the floor trying to catch your breath.
    "You need to leave me alone," I said.
    "I love you," he said.
    "No."

He got off the couch and came to me. He knelt and touched my chin. He wiped a drop of sweat away and smiled. His hand was heavier than it should have been. Too hot. It stopped my lungs and stole away my voice. There were so many things I wanted to say but no words came.

Everything hung on the tips of my teeth.

"I love you," he said.

I tried to push. I tried to fight. Pain etched my bones. I gagged. He held me to the floor with nothing more than his fingertips and his voice. I couldn't move or think or breathe and I thought for sure he was going to kill me, but he didn't. He didn't kill me. He leaned in and kissed me. Even this close, his face was smoky and blurred with a haze like cigarette smoke. I knew the shape of his body and the smell of his breath. I wanted to know if his lips were thick and red or thin and pale. I wanted to know what color his eyes were and if they carried the narrow menace that made his voice so frightening. But it wasn't going to happen. All I knew was that his jaw was long and hard. I knew that his nose was narrow and straight. That was it.

Dread

In the space between sleep and no sleep, I dreamed that Tayla was going to kill me with a straight razor. She chased me back and forth on a bus trying to slit my throat. I dreamed of a hole I kept falling into over and over. I dreamed that a murder of crows was trying to eat my eyes. These were regular dreams, unpleasant, but temporary.

Things changed. Gid lay on my bed with me, his edges faintly wine-colored. Somehow, Tayla'd gone away.

"You did this," he said.
"What does that mean?" I asked.
"I can give you everything." Doubt folded over itself.
"What are you?"
"A man," he said. "More than man."
"Jesus."

Gid smiled and cracked my ribs with his fingers. My heart stopped. He kissed his way down my thighs. My hips cramped. He pushed me into rage and pain. Fear and shame burned me to my bones.

"It hurts," I said.
"You make me," he said. "And I make you."

Twisting away was hard but I did it and then everything came apart. Something moved in me. Something cold. Something hard. It moved through me like cold steel, cutting and tearing.

"I love you," he said.
"I don't believe you," I said.
"Yes, you do," he said.

The words were insane. I ground my fingertips into my palms, frustrated.

"I love you," he said.
"Why?"

Walls vanished. A cool breeze swirled over me, chilling the sweat stuck to my face.

"Why?" I asked aloud.

Tayla grunted in her sleep. I didn't want to wake her. I didn't want her to see me like this. I didn't want the greasy dread in my gut but there was nothing I could do about that. There was nothing I could do at all.

Blurred

Tayla started the coffee. Light from the porch was thin and weak. She turned to me, silent. Her face was stiff and stern, a red and black mask. I tried not to look at her. It was impossible. Her eyes pulled me in, held me. I forgot to breathe for a moment.

"Who's Gid?" she asked.

Her voice ground out like stones in tin bucket. I wanted to tell her. I wanted to explain the whole thing. Gid's voice punched in.

"It's a secret," he said.

I swallowed.

"A guy," I said.

"A guy?" she asked.

"I told you."

"Your dream."

"My dream."

Tayla walked out. She went to the lawn and dug her toes into the muddy grass. I joined her and the cold and the rain hurt my joints, but Tayla simply ignored it.

I thought about Gid. I thought about the blurred face. How come I couldn't see him? Did that mean anything? How do I tell Tayla about it? Will she believe me? Do I?

"I see him sometimes," I said.

"It's just a dream," Tayla said.

"Maybe."

She looks at me with that scared, brave look. It was the look she got when things were slipping away. It was the look she put on when she was doing something she didn't like doing.

"I'm okay," I said.

Doubt. Fear.

"Really?" she asked.

"It'll pass," I said.

I didn't know that for sure. Gid was different. He was more than a dream but less than real. I didn't know what to do with him. All I knew was that I hated everything about him.

Worry sharpened her face. Her eyes narrowed, and her fingers played a silent song on her thigh. Our cigarettes burned down, and we went into the kitchen. Tayla poured us coffee and we sat at the table. She held my hand.

"I'm going to be okay," I said.

I wasn't sure if I was right or not, but saying it meant something. Tayla didn't look sure either. They were just words. No promises. Just hope. We needed it, but neither of us trusted it.

The Object of Envy

Ravens rose on broad black wings into a porcelain sky. Starlings moved in mobs, black specks swirling around like fish. I stood in the muddy path outside the Shack smoking a cigarette. A wet wind promised rain later.

"Hey," Tad said.

I jumped and spun. He backed away, hands up.

"Sorry," he said.

I blinked and all the edges came back. Things went from a mass of colored fields to individual buildings and trees. Grass spread out sharp and sparkling in shafts of sunlight.

"What're you doing?" Tad asked.

"Watching the dance."

A frown formed between his brows but then he looked up. The starlings rippled there and Tad smiled, getting it.

"Cool," he said.

He went in and brought out a couple of lawn chairs.

"Is there music?" he asked.

For a moment, I thought he was mocking me, but when I turned to snap at him, his empty face stopped me.

"Sometimes," I said. "Mostly colors."

I felt his eyes wash over me and I chose to ignore it.

"Tell me," he said.

Something went through me. It was kind of warm and soft.

"Pink streamers," I said. "Piercing green strings. You don't see it?"

He shook his head. A sadness bubbled out of my gut.

"I wish I didn't," I said.

He took my hand.

"Why?"

How do you explain what it was like living in two worlds at once? Things were always so complicated. People were always afraid. I didn't know how to explain the weight of people's eyes.

"I wish," he said. "I wish I saw things more like you." He swallowed and sighed. "Everything's so fake. None of this matters. None of it means anything." I squeezed his fingers. "It would be nice to see pretty things all of the time," he said.

I nearly laughed out loud. Tad was a sweet boy, but he had no idea how hard it was trying to figure out what was really there and what came from my head.

"I'd like to be different than the rest," he said.

I leaned my head on his broad shoulder and let the rest of it go away. We all wanted what we couldn't have. Still, it was nice being the object of envy once.

Unprovoked

A large mirror covered a wall. In it I saw my vast body moving. Angie's slender figure twirled around me. I lifted her and tossed her high. Tayla beat the keys with a vicious temp.

Sweat spun off me in thick drops. My tits felt heavy. My hips were clumsy. It wasn't coming together. I didn't know how to stop though. Inertia pulled me through until Tayla slammed the final chord out. Angie spun to a stop.

"Shit," I said.

I walked to my bag and grabbed a towel. Anger flashed hot and fast. I kicked the bag into the corner. Both Tayla and Angie watched me, silent. They traded looks.

"Fuck," I said.

In a corner of my mind, I knew I was overreacting. I knew this was just a practice and practice was the time to fuck things up. But I couldn't help myself.

I prowled around the room muttering through the silent laughter rising from the floor. I stamped my foot, childish and silly.

"Jesus."

Things split. There were the edges of the walls. The floor was hard and warm on my bare feet. Chairs stood solid in the solid light. But they went kind of hazy too. A paisley film lay over everything, spinning and splitting, meeting like bulbs of floating water. I roared, a gut sound.

"Baby," Tayla said.

"Stop!" I yelled.

Tayla's flinching face, the way Angie enjoyed the show, lit a shameful light in me. Something was wrong. My body was not my body. My thoughts belonged to someone else.

"Did you do this?" I snarled at Tayla.

She put her hands up. Voices screamed at me.

"Shut up!" I bellowed.

Air seemed to slice through me. Part of me hid in a corner of my mind whimpering at me to stop.

"We have to get this right," I said. "Come on."

I held a hand out to Angie. She shook her head.

"Sit down," Tayla said.

Something in her voice told me that she was scared. Tayla was scared. Tayla was never scared.

"Butter," she said. "I have something for you."

It was a threat. I bared my teeth, hissing.

"It'll help," she said.

She came and handed me a pill and a bottle of water.

"You're killing me," I said.

"No," she said. "You know me. I'd never hurt you."

It was a lie. She hurt me all of the time. But she hurt me less than others. She tried not to hurt me. No one else cared enough to try even that much.

"Ativan," Tayla said. "It'll help."

Wrestling with the rage and the powerlessness, I forced the pill into my mouth and washed it down with water. I sucked in a mouthful of warm air and went to the corner. My head dropped to my knees. My arms wrapped themselves around my shins.

Jesus, I thought. *My thighs are fucking huge.*

The only noise for a long time was my raspy breathing.

"I should go," Angie said.

Soft feet walked on the hard floor. A nylon bag groaned.

"Call me," Angie said. "Lock up."

The door creaked a little and sunlight filled the studio for a moment. Tayla came and sat with me.

"You okay?" she asked.

She took my hand.

"We'll get through this," she said.

We? There was no we. There was me and the shit in my head. Tayla had no idea. Still, she tried.

"I'm sorry," I said.
"Me too," she said.
We sat there a long time, waiting for the right moment to get up and pretend nothing happened.

Glass

The room was mine. The walls were blank though. Still, somewhere, something rattled like glass in a wind storm. Naked and cold, I felt the music coming from the walls to rub against my skin like a large, unwanted dog.

The light here was thick, the color of a winter storm, smooth as a marble floor. The bed was where the bed was supposed to be, and I lay on it staring out the window at Mt. Hood. Only Mt. Hood was too far away to see at night. The ceiling, too, was so far above me I couldn't see the webs in the corners.

Gid came. He came from somewhere behind me. I couldn't see his face. I couldn't see his hands. He said nothing. He came to the middle of the room and there was music. Miles Davis blasted the space between us.

"Come," he said.

He reached out and took my hand. I didn't remember reaching for him, but he lifted me to my feet and I lay my head on his chest. Music circled us.

His warm hands wrapped themselves around my waist and held me tight. I knew what was coming. I hated the thought of it. More than anything, I wanted to wake and for it to be over.

Anxiety and nausea flooded through me. I gagged and choked.

"Hush," he said. "You're okay."

How could I be okay? How could this happen to me? Tears rolled from my eyes, little bits of disgust and fear. Gid touched them, one at a time, letting them soak into his fingertips.

When he lifted me up, I twisted and fought a little. His hands squeezed me until I couldn't breathe.

"Hush," he said. "This is going to hurt."

Things got too heavy. Gid kissed my spine, between the shoulder blades. He took me to the bed. When he pushed into me, I screamed. I screamed and screamed. My throat felt as if it were being torn out.

Lights flickered for a moment. Lights and heat and weight lay on me. I opened my eyes and Tayla was there. She held me and whispered something over and over in my ears. Things rang and shuttered. The walls, even with the paintings and posters on them, seemed foreign and strange. I had to move. Tayla held me down.

"Let go," I said over and over. "Let go. Let go. Let go."

"You're okay," Tayla said. "It was only a nightmare."

We lay together for a long time. Tayla whispered in my ear.

"Breathe with me," she said. "In. Out."

I breathed and Tayla's hand got lighter. Things were slowing down.

"It was him," I said.

"Him?"

"Gid."

"Jesus," Tayla said.

Lines formed in her face. She leaned away from me as if I smelled or something.

"It's just a dream," she said.

"He's killing me."

Telling these secrets felt like a betrayal. These dreams, if they were dreams, were mine and mine alone. Talking about them made me all shivery and shameful. My voices hated me. I hated me. Suicidal thoughts filled me up. I saw blood. My wrists itched in anticipation of a blade.

"Look at me," Tayla said.

I couldn't.

"Look," she said.

She grabbed my chin, turning me to face her. When I opened my eyes, she was too far away. The distance between us was uncrossable.

"I love you," she said. Sweet words. Good words. Still, they brought Gid to mind. They crushed through me. Love was a hammer beating me into the ground.

Glorious

Downtown. Sunlight and bricks and glass. I wanted to go home. Too many people filled the sidewalks. Too many cars growled in the streets. It was dangerous. I was exposed and open. My guts rumbled, and my hands shook. I walked with my head down.

"It's okay," Miss Tris said and took my hand.

Tayla and Tad smoked cigarettes, cutting a path through the crowd. People stared. People talked. It was too much.

"I need to go home," I said.

Tayla looked over her shoulder. I saw the frustration there. I saw the anger.

"I'm sorry," I said.

She turned away. Miss Tris squeezed my fingers.

"We're almost done," she said.

She carried clothes in a bag. They talked me into this. They said it would be good for me to get out. They said the only way to deal with fear was to face it. I faced it and it won.

"Breathe," Miss Tris said.

I sucked warm air into my lungs. I lit a cigarette.

We heard the voice before seeing the man. He carried a bullhorn. The words were just part of the world until we rounded the corner. He stood in the middle of the sidewalk with a friend. The friend carried a sandwich board and pamphlets.

"God's hate is divine," the man shouted.

The man with the booklets came to us.

"Repent," he said.

I stepped away. Tayla stepped forward. Tayla always stepped forward.

"Go away," she said.

The man preaching turned to us.

"Turn away from sin," he shouted. "Hate your sin and God will save you." Tad shook his head. Miss Tris tried to lead me around everyone.

"Hating your sin is an act of love," the man shouted. He moved with us. He refused to let us past.

"You're blind to sin," he shouted.

He put his hand on Tayla's shoulder. Tad grabbed him.

"You need to stop," Tad said.

"I am not afraid," the man shouted.

Tayla looked him in the eye and shoved. He stumbled.

"Get away," she said.

The man raised his hands. "This," he shouted, "this is the devil's work on earth!"

It happened too fast. I couldn't stop it. I turned and puked. I puked on the man's shoes.

People stopped. People stared. Miss Tris screamed her laughter. A small cheer went up.

"Are we done?" Tad asked the man.

The man glared at us.

"I think we're done," Tad said.

We moved on. Tad and Tayla draped their arms on my shoulders.

"Did you do that on purpose?" Tayla asked.

I shook my head.

"Still," she said. "Brilliant."

We walked on. I was empty and full at the same time. I was thrilled and ashamed.

Sometimes accidents were divine. Sometimes shame was glorious.

Drinks and Sex

Men came and went. Not real men. These men were drunks. They'd been coming here for years, long before Angie got the bar in her divorce. These old drunks were far gone, sad and empty.

Wasted girls spun on a brass pole with no grace or care. Thin legs barely held them up. Eyes, too big in their sockets, refused to look anyone in the face. They collected their tips and ran away to their dressing room. I only came on the weekend. Angie paid me to clean after hours.

I sat and watched the men and the men watched their drinks. Gid came into my head and whispered secrets, a voice from my dreams.

"They think you're a whore," he said.

He wasn't there, just his voice. I turned my face to a corner and pretended to hear only the music.

"All you have to do is love me," he said.

"Love," I say.

One old man down the bar looked at me with his rheumy eyes. I stared him down and he turned back to his drink.

"You're more than this," Gid said.

A man came and leaned too close. He wore a tie and shirt and slacks. He looked like a car salesman or a teacher or something. He grabbed my hand and pulled me toward him.

"Hands," I said.

"You're a meaty one," he said.

"Stop," I said.

He grabbed my face and kissed my mouth. At first, I didn't know what to do, but then, I bit his lip. He yelped and pushed me away. I fell and his hand went to his bloody mouth. He kicked me in the head. Lights flashed, and the walls spun. Something warm ran from my nose. I spun and curled around myself. He reached down and grabbed my arm. He hauled me to my feet, slapping me. The whole room twisted and I was on the floor again. Angie rushed over with a small bat.

"What the hell?" she asked.

"She bit me," the man said.

"You don't hit my girl," Angie said.

"Bitch."

"Time for you to go," Angie said.

"Damned right."

He stormed out and I got up.

"You okay?" Angie asked.

"Yeah."

"That's going to bruise."

"Sorry."

"Did you really bite him?"

"I'd had enough."

"You can't bite people," she said. "No more biting."

"No promises."

That World

Everything was incomprehensible. Images lay over one another like leaves in summer trees. Things changed without warning, flipping quickly by.

First, I stood on a building, a single black tower in an empty world. The air was perfectly still, poised like a cat just before the pounce.

Next, water brawled by and dropped over an edge, falling forever. Mist and noise fought around me, folding and bawling. The bottom was so far away it lost meaning as soon as realized I wasn't going over.

Things changed again. The ground stretched without end. Stones gathered in sullen groups. Prickly plants muttered and cussed at me. They reached out with sharp fingers to pull at me. Heat and grit ground away until I was nothing but meat. In front of me, a vast hole.

"This is all yours," Gid said.

He came out of the bruised air and stood with me. I tried to cringe but my body wasn't my own.

"Everything else is illusion," he said.

I couldn't speak. Gid kissed me. Everything crumpled.

"You cannot serve two masters," he said, a disembodied voice.

I spun into glittering dust, a single speck wrapped in nothing.

Secrets

Sadness verged on depression. I stood at the edge waiting for one word, one thought to send me over. It was hard to think or even exist. Somehow, I left my body and floated in the corner of the room watching and listening. Everyone here was a cutout. Fake. They stared at Mac with dead eyes. Their thoughts pushed into my head, crowding me. Mac stood at the front of the class talking about *Romeo and Juliet*.

"It wasn't love that killed them," he said. "It was secrecy."

None of it mattered to me. I hated Shakespeare. I hated when people couldn't get to the point. Shakespeare talked around things instead of coming right out and saying what he needed to say.

I sat and listened to the crow in the window talk about the fiery taste of stolen eggs and nestlings. I listened to him bitch about the arrogance of ravens.

"Butter," Mac said.

I jerked back to reality.

"You okay?" Mac asked.

I nodded.

"You were talking to yourself," he said.

Blood flooded my face. This was not good. No one wanted to know what was in my head. It scared them. It embarrassed them. Coy sat in his chair, smirking, whispering something to the guy next to him.

"Do you need a break?" Mac asked.

I gathered my shit and retreated to the hall. I stood alone on the hard floor. The sadness came back though, heavier now, duller: full on depression. I could barely move. Ghosts came from the corners without faces, without hands or feet. Voices screamed. I jumped and twitched. I remembered every sin I'd committed. Shame turned the blood solid in my veins. On the way to the Shack, rain pierced my face and forearms with cold pins. Trees scratched their names on the sky. The birds had all given up and gone home. When would I get to go home?

Real Enough

Orion hung in the southern sky, just west enough to dip his toe into the Coast Range. Somewhere out there, the Pleiades rode Taurus like witches riding dreamers. I couldn't find them though. The moon was small, lopsided. Frogs filled the darkness with their throaty songs. Faces formed in the light from the windows. Dead folks told me things. They called my name.

"It's easy," they said. "Just walk away."

I couldn't though. Everywhere I went, the world followed. This world and the world in my head. Noises and colors lay on everything like leaves rotting in the woods. I closed my eyes and waited.

"Are you coming to bed?" Tayla asked.

I jumped. Tayla had a way of sneaking up on me.

"Butter?"

"He's coming," I said.

"Shit."

Tayla came and put her hand on my back. Tayla had strong fingers. She was a powerful woman.

"Come to bed," she said.

"He's going to hurt me," I said.

Tayla sighed.

"I'm here," she said.

"So is he," I said.

"Butter…"

I spun and stared at her. She stared back. This was not a night to fight. This was not how I wanted the day to end. I went to bed. I followed Tayla to the bathroom. She showered with me as if she was afraid I'd drown myself.

"He's real enough," I said.

"I know," Tayla said.

But she didn't know. She had no idea. No one did. No one knew what it was like to have their dreams come to life.

Escape

Tayla and Angie took me to the Egyptian Room. I'd never been.

"Every Thursday's topless karaoke night," Angie said. "I know the bouncer. She'll let us in."

Tayla and I looked at each other. *Topless Karaoke?* Tayla grinned. She was just glad to get out. She was glad we were doing something. I hated it but I had to do something. I had to give a little back.

Tayla leaned over and kissed me. We made promises with our tongues. It was a night out. It was a chance to get away from craziness, a chance to be young and gay and comfortable. I was more than a little scared.

"It'll be fine," Angie said.

Cool air painted the night a soft rose color. Angie drove, ignoring everything. She rushed yellows and charged reds. She threw profanities like stones.

There was no parking at the Egyptian Room. We left the car down the street and walked back. The Egyptian Room was packed. Women stood shoulder to shoulder, dancing, drinking and smoking, laughing and talking. A tall girl stood on the stage singing Queen's "Fat Bottom Girls."

Angie shrugged out of her shirt and dragged me out to the dance floor. She pressed herself against me. She was firm and slick. Her tits were hard against mine. It was just a dance, but it was more than a dance. Over and over, I looked at Tayla but Tayla was looking elsewhere.

We were together but sometimes Tayla looked. It was harmless.

"Come on," Angie said. "Relax."

I let the music flow through me. I let my heart beat. I sucked the smoky air into my lungs.

Angie leaned in. Her lips traced a small pattern against my neck. This was more than I asked for. I jerked away. Angie laughed.

"It'll be a secret," she said.

We danced and then we went to the bar and drank. The drinks went to my head. The walls spun and the lights boiled through my eyes. Tayla paid no attention when Angie's hands found their way under my shirt.

"Angie!"

"I've seen them before," she said.

"I'm with Tayla," I said.

"And she's right there," Angie said.

The lack of fear scared me. Part of me remembered Angie's body in the shower. Part of me wanted to see what more there was. But this wasn't something I could do. Not with Tayla right there.

Last call came. Angie shrugged into her shirt. We drove home. Night folks stood on corners, but they meant nothing. Lights flashed, and trees blurred. Tayla's hand caressed my thigh. Nights like this fired her up.

The city gave way to hills and the hills to small towns. Angie shot through the back roads with a wildness that scared me.

"Angie," I said.

"I have it," she said.

Gravity pulled me in too many directions. I leaned in my seatbelt. We squealed around a corner. Red and blue lights behind us.

"Shit," Angie said and stomped the gas.

We took the corner to our street and before I could think, we were parked.

"Inside," Angie said. "Go. Inside. Now."

We ran over the yard. The cop tore onto our street.

"Hide!" Angie snapped.

We crouched behind a hedge. The cop slowed but didn't stop. My lungs ached. Angie and Tayla choked on their laughter. As soon as the cop was gone, Angie pulled me into the house. Angie and Tayla bent with laughter and excitement.

"Jesus," I said.

Angie danced around. Fear turned her on.

"Prepare yourself," she said.

She kissed Tayla and then she kissed me. Tayla went with it.

"Is this happening?" I asked.

Tayla looked at me with bright eyes.

"You ready?" she asked.

Angie cupped my tits. It was happening. We kissed and we spun and we fell into bed. We bent and swirled and ate each other alive.

Promises

Gid stared at me and I stared at him.
"I'll give you everything," he said.
"What is this?" I asked.

The room was too large. The moon in the sky shouldn't have been there but it was hanging cold and distant and indifferent. Purple shadows ate the echoes.

Something vague and scary pressed down on me. I rose too fast, too hard into an endless sky. Everything tilted and the dream petered out. I lay in bed and listened to Tayla breathe. She opened her eyes and stared at me.

"What're you doing?"
"Waiting," I said.
"Fuck."

She sat up and wrapped her arms around her knees. Wild hair flared around her head like a halo. Some of it stuck to her face, sweat wet and oily looking.

"Something's going to happen," I said.

It was. I could feel it coming. The air tasted of static and ozone. My hands wavered on my wrists.

"Go back to sleep," Tayla said and rolled away.

I lay down and closed my eyes. Sleep teased me. Fragments of words spun through my head. Parts of a room. Faces and hands. Hints of movement prickled along the nerves.

"Stop," I said.

Out of nowhere, Gid laughed.

Shit Follows

Voices told me to run. If I went somewhere where no one knew me, maybe the voices would fade, and I'd be normal. If only for a day.

"I want to go away," I said.

"Go away?"

"You know," I said. "Somewhere new."

Tayla sighed and steered around a silver CRV. A couple of older women sat in the front talking. They looked good together, like they had a history. I wondered if they were a couple. I wanted to know everything about them, but they fell away and Tayla turned toward home.

"Nothing's going to change," she said.

I nodded.

"Shit follows," she said.

I knew it. I knew she hated me. I knew she was going to leave. I popped the door open.

Asphalt sped by. Cars honked. Tayla swerved.

"Jesus!" she shouted.

She got to the curb, her fingers white on the wheel.

"What the fuck?" she screamed.

Jamming the car into park, she grabbed my arm, tight, too tight. I pulled.

"Stop!" I yelled.

"Butter, goddammit."

We wrestled for a moment, pulling and pushing. I had to get out. I had to get away. A wild, fiery fear filled me. I fought with the seatbelt latch. Tayla slapped at me, cussing and blocking my fists as I tried to punch her. She was going to kill me. She was going to hide the body in the woods and no one would ever see me again.

The seatbelt gave way and I jumped onto the sidewalk. I ran but my feet were too heavy and the air hammered on me. I wasn't fast enough. Tayla caught me. She grabbed my shirt and tossed me into a yard. Grass jabbed at my back, wet and sharp.

"Butter!" Tayla screamed. "Butter! Stop!"

Everything spun me, too bright and too hard. Tayla knelt next to me, stroking my face.

"Butter," she said. "You're okay."

"No."

"Remember," Tayla said. "Come back."

Gid was there. He stood wrapped in royal shadows. He nodded to me and pressed one finger to his lips. I stood there and stared at him and he came to me.

"Do you see him?" I asked.

I knew then that he was there to kill me. He was going to tear my heart out.

I looked from Tayla to Gid. Gid held out a hand. Something pulled at me. I wanted to go to him. I wanted to run away.

"Butter," Tayla said. "Nothing's there."

I sat in the grass with my head in my hands. I moaned and Tayla wrapped me in her arms.

"You're okay," she said. "No one's going to hurt you."

She was wrong. She knew nothing. I pulled away. I shuddered, and I closed my eyes. I ground my teeth. Tears burned over my cheeks. Snot ran thick and cold from my nose. I was completely out of control. Tayla took my face in her hands.

"You're okay," she said.

But I wasn't. My heart thundered under my ribs. I gagged and choked. The world leaned in over me. Light cut into my eyes like ground glass. Tayla held my hands and rubbed my back.

Everything spun and dipped. Gid came and stood over me whispering secrets.

"You're dying," he said.

Spots bloomed and broke in my eyes. Tayla rose. Monsters came. Monsters with long, mean faces and hands large enough to crush my skull. I tried to run again, but Tayla tripped me up. I fell to the ground.

"No," I screamed. "No, no, no."

"Butter," Tayla said. "Baby. It's okay."

I fought and the monsters flipped me over. They knelt on my back. They pulled my arms out of their sockets and latched steel bracelets on my wrists. Bones grated. Tendons stretched.

More monsters. More words. More people staring.

"Don't resist," the monsters said. "Hold still."

They stood over me. Sunlight burned away the madness. It burned Gid into a shadow.

Slowly, things fell into place. I went still. I breathed and breathed. The cuff's bite brought everything into focus.

"Can I sit up?" I asked.

Tayla looked at the monsters and the monsters became cops. They looked like they hated the idea.

"She's better now," Tayla said.

"Are you sure?" one asked.

"She's better," Tayla repeated.

They let me sit up. People gathered to watch. One of the cops turned to the crowd.

"Enjoying the show?" he asked.

They went away. It didn't matter. I couldn't see them through the tears.

Taking Charge

I lost my mind. Faces roared in the paint. Their teeth gnarled and ground sounding like bones going to dust. Voices whispered plans and painted images. Gore covered everything. Ash and fire ruined my lungs. Black lines rose from the floor, edged with threats and promises.

Mildew stains ran dark in the corners. Mold swayed in the toilet. The razor pulled blood through white fat. It dripped from my fingertips and ran in streaks and rivulets into the drain. I turned on the water and watched it go from red to pink.

Suddenly I was lightheaded. I breathed through my nose. I wasn't done yet. I wanted to cut through muscle to the veins; I wanted to see bone. But I couldn't do it. The pain was starting now and little spots sprouted in my eyes. I let the razor bounce in the sink. I was finished. I started to lie down in the bathtub when the door opened. Tayla stood there, staring. Her mouth worked but nothing came out. After a second, she hit me and started cussing.

"What the hell?" she said.

"Jesus Christ," I said.

I closed my eyes. I didn't know what else to do. All the noise, all the spinning and all the fear drained away for a moment. All the colors went white, then black. I floated.

"Fuck," Tayla said. "Fuck. Fuck. Fuck."

Gid reached into my head but found nothing to hold onto. His finger slipped and scrambled.

"Why?" he asked.

"I made you," I said.

"No."

"You made me," I said.

A shrill scream. Gid or Tayla. It didn't matter. I was done.

Emergency

Darkness. Thick, vast and utterly absolute. I hung in the void. The edge where flesh met world blurred. I hung there and waited for the universe to explode into sound and motion. I hung there for an eternity and then it happened and when it happened I jerked. Everything jumped at once and then the sounds of the world flooded through. There were voices, no words but the hum of too many people talking at once. Machines tapped out rhythms. Wheeled carts clacked on hard floors. Colors unfolded in my eyes. I tried to turn but something held me down.

Slowly, I opened my eyes and I knew where I was. I was in the emergency room. Acoustic tiles stretched from wall to wall. No windows, only florescent light. Leather cuffs held my wrists to my side, my ankles to the bed frame. Tayla's voice rolled over me.

"There you are," she said,

She leaned in over me. Lines ran out from the corners of her eyes. Her lips were thin and too pale. I turned away. Shame filled the hollow spots in my bones. It soured my stomach.

"What do you remember?" Tayla asked.

"I died."

"You didn't die," she said.

"Okay."

"You know he's not real," she said.

"Can I have my hands back?" I asked.

A frown creased her mouth. She looked out at the hall.

"I need to pee."

"Butter…"

"Please."

She looked unsure for a moment before working on the buckles. Leather separated. I rose slowly and stumbled into the bathroom. It was all pale walls and porcelain. Metal knobs stuck up from the sink. A call button hung from the wall waiting for something awkward to happen.

I peed, and just sat there. Alone. Scared. Sad.

Tayla tapped on the door. I wasn't ready yet, but I couldn't keep hiding. Tayla stood near the bed. Nerves rattled. Breathing deep, moving slowly I sat in the chair in the corner and put my head in my hands.

"You okay?" Tayla asked.

She put her head against mine. Her breath tickled the little hairs on my neck. I wanted to go home. I wanted to get out of here.

"I'm sorry," I said.

We sat together, and the silence folded over us. The weight of her eyes was more than I could take.

"I'm okay," I said.

"Are you?" Tayla asked.

I held my breath.

"I will be," I said.

"Really?"

The anger came back glittering in the air between me us. I swallowed and shivered.

"Yeah," Tayla said. "I thought so.

Friends

Miss Tris and Tad came with flowers.
"You look so sad," Tad said.
Miss Tris held my hand.
"Jesus," she said. "That's nice." Tad flushed.
"It's okay."
Large windows at the end of the hall looked out over the west hills and the freeway. Tad went and pressed his hand to the glass.
"No jumping," I said.
Tad flinched. I hated it. Awkwardness was a hair coat on all of us.
"We love you," Miss Tris said. "This is just a hiccup." Tad nodded. None of us believed it though. This was my life.
"This Gid," Miss Tris said.
Another flinch. They knew things I wished they didn't.
"Tayla told us," Tad said.
"Does he treat you right?" Miss Tris asked.
I shook my head.
"He's real," I said.
"If he's real to you," Tad said. "He's real to us."
It was sweet. It was nice. It was also a complete lie.

Laps

Walls the color of eggshells hemmed me in. Every room had a wooden door, thick, no locks. The only locks were on the nurses' station and the door to the real world. In my room, a window took up most of a wall. It refused to open, but you could see the west hills, bristled with evergreens. Lights from too many houses glowed there at night.

The only thing I could do was walk. Seventeen laps made a mile. I walked three, maybe four miles a day. My staff walked with me. Selma was a short, bulgy woman. Old. Curly white hair. She used a walker, but she never asked to sit down. She walked with me and we talked.

"How're things?" she asked.

I shrugged.

"You seem a little worried," she said.

Again, I shrugged. Selma knew things. She said things. She knew how to get into my head and ferret things out. Gid walked with us, an eggplant smear. He whispered things. His fingers stroked the knobs of my spine.

Nausea and pain played tug of war.

"She doesn't believe," Gid said.

"You're awfully pale," Selma said.

Gid put his hand in the center of my chest. My sternum iced over. I stopped. Selma wheezed to my side.

"You okay?" she asked.

Gid stood with us, blurred and gray. His fingers were hard and strong. I remembered the feel of his broad chest, his rigid thighs.

"She knows nothing," he said.

"Don't."

"Butter?" Selma asked.

"Never mind."

At the corner, I sat in a hard chair.

"She can't help," Gid said.

I shuddered and put my forehead against my knees and tried to breathe. I wanted to puke. I wanted a cigarette. Selma watched me. It was hard to breathe. My feet and fingers tingled. Out of nowhere, blood flowed from the walls and windows. People cried gory tears. Fire raced through the nerves and bones.

Gid stroked my hair. I batted at him but he only laughed.

"They know nothing about love," he said.

He kissed my chin and he kissed my nose. He kissed my forehead and my knuckles.

"You're so sweet," he said.

"Don't," I said. "You can't be here."

"Because they can't see me?"

"You're hurting me," I said.

"Pain cleans the soul."

Burning Sin

Pain shaped my dreams. My wrists screamed as if the bones burned. Something like a nail pierced my feet. A blade of indigo light entered my side under the ribs. Blood washed over my tight, pale skin. I hung in an empty sky.

Gid came and stood below me, looking at my face. I couldn't scream. I twisted and bit my lips. He stared at me and I knew he could have brought me down, but he wouldn't.

"This is necessary," he said.

Necessary? What did I do to need this?

He held his hand under me and caught the blood flowing from me and lifted it to his lips. He drank, and I imagined his red stained lips. If I could only see his face, I would have understood this a lot better. Now, though, I hung here and tried to breathe.

"We're burning sins," he said.

Sins?

"All you have to do is ask," he said.

Ask? Ask what?

Light changed, and the sky folded in on itself turning dark as a bruise. Blind, I rose. Blind, I flew. Somehow, the pain seeped away. Red and green and silver ghosts cut through my eyelids. Somewhere, I heard music. Slowly, I rose out of sleep. I rolled onto my side and puked on the sheets. Memories of the pain, the dream, tingled in my wrists, my feet, my ribs. I sucked wind into my lungs and cried for a moment. He was gone. I was alone.

Awkward

Everyone stared at Angie and she stared back, fearless and fierce. Bright pink light hung on her in flowing streams. She was a great goddess of sex and violence. She stood tall in the world, looking down at the rest of us. She moved through the world with a face filled with cruelty and laughter.

She was a friend, but not a real friend. She lived on the edge of my life. We danced together. Once, Tayla and I fucked her. A mistake. It made things weird.

And now I was shy. I was embarrassed. But here she was.

When she found me, she smiled with sharp teeth. My legs fluttered. She came and hugged me.

"Hey," she said.

"Hey."

She looked around and frowned.

"This place," she said.

I nodded and took her hand. I had to get her out of the hall. She twirled her head as I led her to my room.

"I heard you had a thing," she said.

I nodded.

"Was it bad?" she asked.

"Kind of."

She went to the window and looked out at the spikey green hills on the other side.

"This is kind of pretty," she said.

She tapped the glass with a fingernail.

"Shatter proof?" she asked.

"I guess."

She turned to me.

"Suicide," she said. "Really? Again?"

"Sorry."

Pity and a touch of disgust stained her face for a moment.

"Well," she said, "you made it."

Suddenly, I needed to sit. I needed to lie down. Nausea and shame churned through me.

"Are you okay?"

I nodded but Angie saw more than I wanted her to.

"Listen," she said. "Let me know when you get home. I have some thoughts for the next show."

"Okay."

An eyebrow lifted. A hand rose for a moment before dropping. She hugged me.

"Get better," she said and walked out.

I stood there a long time. I stood there feeling naked, like a monkey in a zoo, making everyone laugh. I stood there a long time and told myself I'd done nothing wrong. It was a lie and I wasn't buying.

The Dead

On the edge of sleep, just before I woke, I found myself standing in the middle of the room, but I wasn't standing in the middle of the room. I was in bed. I saw my body there. This was my room. These were the walls and these were the drawings I'd hung there. These were my windows looking out at the hills. But then, this was not my room. The walls were too far away. The windows were dark and there was no noise from my neighbors or the traffic on the street.

The walls turned pale and the windows closed and merged. Above me, the ceiling arced and disappeared. Light thinned and I was alone. Music came from nowhere and it rasped through my legs, my ribs and head. Slowly, I spun and then I danced. It felt good.

When I stopped, my legs quivered and my lungs bellowed. And then, the world shifted again and I stood there. Dead folks hung from short, black ropes. They hung in shades of lavender. Their bulging eyes were white as boiled eggs. Their purple tongues hung from pale lips, swollen and slick as slugs. I would have left, but there was no path, no gap big enough to get through.

I spun in place, careful not to touch anything. There was only enough room for me. Somehow, I knew the people hanging there. I knew their faces. I knew their hands and the way their hips sloped into their legs. Something told me that these people where part of me and a panic built in my belly, scratching along my spine.

Gid came up behind me. I tried to turn, but his hands held my hips. His voice whispered in my ears.

"These are my dead," he said.

I stared at the bodies. There were so many of them. The dead hanging there marked an eternity of something.

"None of them," Gid said. "Not one of them loved me with perfect faith."

"When they lay on their death beds," he said, "they prayed to me to give them more time. They prayed for immortality."

"Mortal love," he said. "Mortal love only lasts as long as the mortal shell lives."

I didn't know what he wanted. I didn't know what any of this meant. I tried to close my eyes. I told myself this was only a dream, that I could wake up and none of this would mean anything. I focused on trying to pry my eyes open. Light played through here, but there were no shadows. Gid laid his hands flat on my belly and pulled me tight to his hot chest.

"Stop," I said.

I jerked, and I fought. My body broke apart. I was dust. I floated. I faded. I disappeared on an invisible wind.

Real and Not Real

Visiting hours started at six. For ninety minutes, I could pretend I wasn't locked up. For ninety minutes, the world didn't seem so heavy.

I stood in the hallway waiting for Tayla to come through the door. I stood there and waited. It was 6:05. Eighty-five minutes left. Worry made me shaky and anxious. What if she didn't show up? She had to show up. I couldn't stand the thought of having to watch everyone else with their friends and family sitting around the tables in the common room talking like this was just another place in the world.

6:08. Eight minutes late. Selma came and stood with me for a moment.

"She'll be here," she said.

I'd started to worry that maybe Tayla'd been in a wreck. The car could have rolled into a ditch somewhere. She could be lying on the highway out there bleeding and I wouldn't know it for hours.

Selma put her hand on my shoulder.

"Breathe," she said.

I sucked air into my lungs and ran my hands through my hair. I waited, but then there she was. I saw her through the narrow window in the door leading to the real world. I saw her putting her wallet in a locker. My belly flipped.

Tayla came through the door and I rushed into her arms. Tears fell, and I thought I'd collapse with the relief. Tayla held me and let me cry. No one said anything, and we stood there like that for a long time. We stood there until I felt like I could walk and breathe again. Once I was okay, she stood back and looked at me.

"You're so pretty," Tayla said.

She kissed my forehead.

"How're things?"

"Same."

"Want to go to your room?" she asked.

Walking to my room, it felt like everyone stared at us. They were crafty though. Whenever I spun around, trying to catch someone staring, no one paid us any attention. Tayla eyeballed me. She didn't want to say anything. She wanted to act like everything was normal, but nothing was normal.

"You okay?" Tayla asked.

I shrugged and looked into the corner, waiting for Gid to come make this visit miserable.

He didn't though.

"I'm feeling better," I said.

"I brought your homework," Tayla said. "I gave it to the nurse."

"Okay."

"Are you sleeping?"

"Off and on," I said.

Tayla put her arm around me. She looked around the room, picking her words as if they were precious. She was working up to something.

"Is he here?" she asked.

"Gid?"

"Gid."

"Not right now," I said. "He comes and goes."

"You know he's not real, right?"

"He's real enough. Just because you can't see him doesn't mean he's not real."

"That's exactly what it means," Tayla said.

I swallowed and looked away. She took my face in her hands and stared into my eyes. It was all very intense.

"What's he look like?" Tayla asked\.

"He's tall, broad-shouldered."

"What color are his eyes?"

I stared at the trees on the other side of the window.

"He's very handsome," I said.

"I'm sure."

"Violet," I said. "His eyes are violet. Like Liz Taylor."

It was a guess. His voice told me his face was square, clean shaven, strong. His hands told me his eyes were violet.

"Maybe you'll meet him," I said.

"This is weird," Tayla said.

"I'll introduce you."

"Maybe if you knew what he looked like," she said.

"Maybe then, he'd be real."

"He's hurting you," Tayla said.

"Sometimes," I said.

"This isn't real," Tayla said.

"Nothing's real," I said.

"You know better than that," Tayla said.

"Maybe," I said. "Maybe not."

Release

They sent me home. It was morning and I stood in the lobby waiting. I wanted a cigarette. I wanted to feel the wind on my face. In just a few minutes, I'd be out. No one could stop me. So I stood at the door and I waited. My fingertips scrubbed at the seam of my jeans.

Nurses and techs, other people, the crazy people wandered around. No Gid.

Maybe he's gone, I thought.

I wanted to be back to a normal life. I wanted to be the normal crazy girl. I wanted to be alone in my head.

Through the window in the door, I saw Tayla. She waved and when she came in, I rushed into her arms.

"Ready?" Tayla asked.

We gathered my things and we went down the hall to the elevator. The closer we got to the parking lot, the more I wanted a cigarette. As soon as we cleared the doors, I lit up.

We walked to the car. Ash filled my lungs. Tayla watched me, measuring my madness. She watched but said nothing.

We drove pasted trees, glass buildings and cars. We held hands.

"Are you ready for this?" she asked.

I nodded. I was. I was ready for anything.

Home

Part of me thought things would be different. I mean, I'd been gone for a long time. The world had spun too many times. But nothing had changed. The walls were the same ivory color. The photos were in the same frames they'd been in for years. Even the voices I heard whispered their familiar messages.

I came into the living room and stood for a moment taking everything in. Tayla came up behind me and wrapped her arms around my waist. She kissed the back of my neck.

"You okay?" she asked.

I nodded. I was home. Everything was fine. I shivered when Tayla's hand rose from my hips to my tits. She kissed my neck again and rested her forehead against the back of my skull. I turned and found her lips. She tasted of cigarettes and cinnamon.

Our room was down the hall. Walking was a little hard with Tayla stroking my ribs, pressing herself against my spine. We fell on the bed. It wasn't long before we were naked and wet. We stroked and bit and kissed. We licked and used our fingers to lift each other into the hazy light. I felt almost human again.

The Edge of Dreams

No sleep. Every night I walked to the edge of dreams, but I never jumped in. I lay in bed listening to the world. Dogs barked and whined. Cars growled on the street like angry cats. The oak outside the window sang a sad song in the wind.

After an hour or two, I got up and went out for a cigarette. I stood on the patio and watched the sun come up over Mt. Hood and I nearly cried with fatigue.

I sat on the couch in a haze. Nothing got to me. I went to school and danced, and no one bothered me. Talking became too much work. Thinking became too hard. It was easier to just float through life as if it were nothing more than water.

School ended and I went home and I lay on the couch in the living room. Before I knew it, I slept. I dreamed. The dream was weird, all lavender light and wind. I rose up out of myself and spun in the air. Music from nowhere seeped through everything. It pushed me higher and higher. Gid stood behind me.

"There's a better life for you," he said. "I can give you everything."

"I don't want anything," I said.
"You need to choose," he said. "Here or not here."
"Stop," I said.
Gid laughed.
"Just stop."
Gid's hot hands crawled up through me. I twisted away but it was too late. He'd already taken hold of me. His dry lips slithered on my throat, against my ear. His tongue rested on the back of my neck.
"I love you," he said.
I pushed him away. I hit him, and I screamed.
"Leave!" I screamed. "Just go!"

He was a wall of bone and muscle. He was a well of arrogance. He sucked me in. I was disappearing. Darkness swallowed me. I couldn't breathe.

I woke, scared and sweaty. Tayla murmured in her sleep. "No," she said. "Stop."

For once, she sounded scared. For once, she was on the bottom of things.

"Not even she knows," Gid whispered in my head.

He had a hold on me. I couldn't get free. I was meat, a fantasy, a dream.

I was an object.

A Brittle Moment

It came all at once. It came out of nowhere. I was both eternal and finite. I was immortal, and death was imminent. My head swam. Fear fought with calm.

"Butter," Tayla said. "What're you doing?"

"What?"

"Your hands are bleeding."

I held them up. Small pools of blood gathered in my palms. Now that I saw them, I felt the pain. The wounds were shallow, nothing more than deep scratches. Still, I couldn't remember doing it.

"What're doing?" Tayla asked again.

I shrugged.

"Jesus," she said. "Wash your hands."

In the bathroom, blood pinked the cold water. It stung. I had no sense of time. Even now, I was not in my body. I was off somewhere watching all of this happen. Tayla came to the bathroom door.

"You're hurting yourself again," she said.

There was an accusation there.

"Sorry."

"What's going on?" she asked.

"I don't know."

"You can't keep doing this," she said.

"What do you want me to say?"

She shook her head and walked away. I looked in the mirror. I hated mirrors. I hated the way my face stopped making sense when I saw it. This was not how I saw myself.

"Tayla," I called.

"What?"

She sounded bitter.

"I didn't do it on purpose," I said.

She came back to the bathroom.

"I know," she said.

"Why are you mad then?" I asked.

She looked at the floor. She looked at the ceiling.

"It's not easy," she said.

"Tell me about it," I said.

She closed her eyes.

"Can we just forget about it?" she asked.

I nodded. I would love to forget about it. I would love to forget everything.

Date Night

Tayla stood at the stove. She refused to let me help.
"This is special," she said. "Go away."
Nerves shimmered through me but Tayla was stern. This was her being nice. It didn't happen a lot. Not that Tayla wasn't kind, but most of the time her kindness came with an edge.
I needed to do something, so I walked around the house. Everything was familiar but meaningless. It was like when I stared at a mirror too long. Sometimes my face fell apart leaving me with nothing but jagged pieces. A cheekbone. A nose. An eye. I knew the ivory walls rising around me. I recognized the photos and paintings, but they made no sense.
"These things," Gid said, "are things. They will fade."
I closed my eyes and pushed him out of my head. Even so, the words stuck. Even running a finger along the edges of a framed photo of Tayla and me at the beach did nothing to reassure me.
Tayla called me into the kitchen to try the caramelized onions and blueberry topping she'd made for the pork. I didn't know where the money came from and didn't ask. The topping was good if a bit too sweet. Tayla took my hand, shocking me back into the world. I pulled away, startled, and went back to the living room.
Tayla finished cooking and brought the meal to the table. She lit candles and poured wine. She fixed a plate for me, three pieces of pork and red potatoes. She piled salad on the side. I waited until she was ready before digging in. It was delicious. Sometimes, Tayla surprised me with her domestic skills. Cooking and cleaning were not things she did often but when she did them, she did them with skill and drive.
Tayla reached across the table and took my hand.
"Dance with me?" she asked.
It was weird. Tayla didn't dance. I shrugged. Things were happening here and I had no idea what was coming.

Tayla put on Duke Ellington. We held each other and swayed to the rhythm. Everything faded away. All I knew was that Tayla and I were here. Something warm washed through me. Tayla stared at me and smiled. Resting my head on hers, I let things happen without worrying why or how, without thought.

But then Gid came.

"It won't last," he said.

I shuddered and held tight. Maybe if I held on tight enough, Tayla would chase Gid away. I doubted it, but it was my only hope.

Tragic Morning

Trees on the edge of town reached up and scratched the sky. The sky screamed. Rain fell like linen in the window. I walked in the cemetery on the hill. Lights from town filled the valley with thin light. I sat amongst the tombstones with the dead. I wondered about them, what they thought, what they did. I let them run their fingers along the edges of my flesh.

I wondered about death. Not enough to kill myself, but enough to get close, to hear the voices, to see the faces. Sometimes, I took too many pills and floated in the room waiting for someone to come lead me away. No one ever came.

I lit a cigarette and started down the hill. The asphalt road glittered in the winter night like crushed glass. A car rolled by, music echoing from the windows. I walked, and the town rose over me with its sharp edges and hard planes.

Sunrise was more than two hours away. School would open, and I'd have to go back to pretending that I wasn't the crazy, fat girl. I'd have to pretend that I was invisible while everyone stared at me.

Cars filled the streets. People were going to work or coming home. Fog and mist haloed their lights. I was all wrapped up in my head. I stepped off the curb and then it happened. First, the horn hit me. Loud. Futile. Then the bumper. It felt as if the world twisted for a moment. I looked up and the sky looked back. I didn't know what had happened. Suddenly, faces loomed over me. They looked scared. They were pale and narrow in the light from the streetlamps.

"Are you okay?" people asked. "Can you move?"

I tried to move, the pain blinded me. My leg throbbed, and my hands stung. Something warm ran from my nose. Darkness fluttered at the edges of everything. I tried to move again, and it gulped me down. That was it. This was the end. Maybe now, things would go my way.

Between Here and There

"What do you see?" Gid asked.

Cold darkness. Towers of bruised rock. A sun gone small and unsympathetic.

"Butter," Gid said. "What do you see?"

"I'm dead."

"Not completely," he said.

I thought of *The Princess Bride* and smiled.

"I feel dead."

Something stroked my bones, reminding me that not even sleep stopped all of the pain.

"Are you an angel?" I asked.

He stood with me, tall and limned with light.

"No."

"What then?" I asked.

"You," he said.

"What?"

"Never mind," he said.

A crash of air and stone. An explosion of light. Things spun, and I lost track of everything.

Worry

Broken leg. Broken ribs. Dislocated shoulder. Road rash and concussion.

Tayla touched my face.

"What were you doing?"

"Walking."

She shook her head.

"You can't just leave like that," she said.

"I came back."

"You could've died."

"Yeah," I said. "That would've been something."

Knives and Sadness

Lying alone in my bed, my leg in a cast, my shoulder braced. The doctor told me not to move around too much with my broken ribs. Moss and ice water packed my head.

Music arced through the house, brittle as lightning. It was too fast to be pleasant.

Discordant and loud. Even with the walls between us and oxy's opiate haze, the chords jarred. Tayla beat the notes with brutal hands. I pictured her at her piano, rod stiff. Her fingers stabbed instead of flowed.

All day she'd been silent and surly, angry about something, but I didn't know what. I was high and sore so I lay in bed and watched the music make fiery colors in the air. I dozed and floated and dreamed forgettable dreams until someone knocked on the door. Sudden silence slapped me. Voices, real voices, not the ones in my head, came down the hall.

Tayla opened the door.

"You have visitors," she said.

Miss Tris and Tad came in. Warm relief softened everything. They came and sat on the bed. Tayla slipped away. I watched her go, trying to figure out the words that would make things okay again, finding nothing but static and jagged sounds. Tad and Miss Tris watched her go with strained eyes but said nothing.

"Jesus, girl," Tad said. "You look like you forgot to bounce." Miss Tris kissed my forehead.

"You're so pretty in your flowery pjs," she said.

"Tayla's pissed," I said.

Tad took my hand.

"You scared us," he said.

"Didn't mean to," I whimpered.

"It's okay," Miss Tris said.

"She hates me," I said, sounding small and weak in my own ears.

"No."

I cried. Thick tears fell from my burning eyes.

"I'm trying," I said.

Tad and Miss Tris held me, one on each side.

"It's not my fault," I said.

They made gentle noises.

"I don't know what to do," I said.

"Get better," Tad said.

"She's just tired," Miss Tris said.

I hoped that was it. I hoped it was just fear and fatigue and not the start of Tayla walking away.

Prayer

"Dear Jesus," I prayed.

"Christ," Tayla said.

We were in the living room. I lay on the couch, floating on oxy.

"I have to," I said.

Tayla rubbed my toes at the end of the cast. She shrugged.

"Dear Jesus," I said.

I was not prone to prayer. If there was a god, he wanted nothing to do with me. Still, something to told me to pray.

"This is stupid," Tayla said.

"Dear Jesus."

Tayla's fingers were hard and strong. Her face was all shadows.

"What should I pray for?" I asked.

"Money."

"Seriously," I said.

"Prayer's not going to do anything," she said.

I closed my eyes again and tried to imagine God. All I saw was Gid. All I knew was that redemption hurt. Pain and fear were my redeeming qualities.

Soon

I knew things. I knew someday Tayla would walk away. Someday, Coy would come with his knife and split me open. I knew I was dying. The couch was hard under me. The cushions were too full. My back hurt. My leg ached.

Gid stood in the corner. Not his usual solid self. The edges of his body were hazed, like ink dropped into water.

"I'm here," he said.

The room was dark. Light from the lamp on the corner fell through the window.

"You're going to be fine," he said.

"I'm dying," I said.

He shook his head.

"I'm scared," I said.

"Scared is good," he said.

I reached for the lamp.

"Don't," he said.

"Gid…"

"Not now," he said. "Not yet."

"I need to see you."

He shivered.

"I'm not ready," he said.

I lay on the couch, heavy and soft. Even the air seemed to press on me.

"Soon?" I asked.

Gid nodded.

"When?" I asked.

"When I'm done," he said.

Between one thought and the next, I slipped away. I fell into thick and seamless dark. I floated.

"When I'm done," Gid said again.

"Soon?"

"Soon enough."

Open Communication

Pain and oxy stretched everything into frayed strings. Colors muted. Sounds echoed and spun into white noise. Miss Tris sat at the end of the couch rubbing my toes. Sometimes they went numb and Miss Tris was willing to squeeze the blood back into them. She took turns with Tayla and Tad taking care of me because I was broken and needed someone to sit with me all of the time.

When she was with me, Miss Tris told me stories from school. She told me about Jessica Barber, the cheerleader, the abstinence-only girl.

"Her water broke right there in bio," Miss Tris said.

I laughed.

"I was a little stoned," she said. "Thought the whole thing was a trick."

"No one knew?" I asked.

"No one."

"How do you not know you're pregnant?" I asked.

"Shame."

I shook my head.

The door boomed open. I jumped and winced. My ribs hurt all of the time, even with the pills, and my shoulder flared when I moved too fast. Even Miss Tris looked scared for a moment. When Tayla saw our faces, she stopped and frowned. Books and groceries filled her arms. A loaf of bread fell to the floor.

"Shit," she said.

Miss Tris got the loaf for her. Tayla nodded at her and they walked into the kitchen. I tried to listen and their words came back mumbled and blurred, tense. Anxiety buzzed along my spine.

"Okay!" Tayla snapped.

A long silence. When Tayla came, her face was carved and pale. Miss Tris came with her own strained mask. Colors brightened. Ivory lined green banners wriggled from the walls and wrapped themselves around my throat. They sat with me.

"We need to talk," Tayla said.

Fear turned the air to a stone in my throat. Tears burned from tired eyes. Numbness spread from fingertips to my palms. The room turned blue then red and finally settled on a sickly purple. Figures formed and unformed in a thick mist.

"Okay," I said, stunned at the calm.

Miss Tris stood and watched. Her body lost depth. She was a shadow of herself.

"This is hard," Tayla said.

No, I thought. *Not this. Not now.*

"She's going to hurt you," Gid whispered, invisible but there, like the smell of roses rotting.

"I'm scared," Tayla said.

All of the tightness left her face. Lines eased. Tears rolled over sharp bones.

"You could've died," she said.

"I didn't mean it," I said.

Both Tayla and Miss Tris scrubbed at their faces with trembling fingers.

"You went away," she said.

"This is it," Gid said.

"You almost didn't come back," Tayla said.

I took her hand.

"You can't do that," she said. "You can't let the world, you can't — you can't let the crazy — you can't leave me."

Colors lost their fiery brightness. Air turned back to air. I pulled Tayla in tight. Pain glittered through me, but I held on anyway.

"Jesus," Tayla said.

"I told you," Miss Tris said.

Tayla gave her the finger. I grinned. Miss Tris laughed and went to the kitchen.

"Are you okay?" I asked.

Tayla rubbed the last of the moment from her eyes. She nodded and things went from broken to a euphoric brittle. Tayla rose.

"Dinner," she said, shrugging herself back into the world.

A lightness lifted me a little but only for a minute.

"She's lying," Gid said.

All the fear and doubt rushed back in, ruining a perfectly good buzz.

Back Again

Voices filled the cafeteria with too much noise. It arced and rolled like stones rattling on a tin roof. Walking was hard and slow. Tayla and I were the last to Queertopia. We shuffled through the crowd to our table. Miss Tris and Tad waited for us there. They had our food and a lacey cloth draped over the table.

"The pretty girl is back!" Miss Tris yelled. "With her Sherpa."

Tayla frowned at her.

"I'm no Sherpa," she said.

On the best of days, the cafeteria seats were miserable; now with my broken bones and my bruises, with my abrasions and strains, they turned tortuous. Still, I sat and sighed. Anything was better than trying to stay upright.

"How're you feeling?" Tad asked.

I shrugged. I hurt. The oxy helped but not enough.

Lunch was greasy burritos and limp lettuce the school claimed was salad. I ate and watched everyone in the room. They talked and laughed, and no one seemed to pay me the slightest attention. All day I heard about my supposed suicide attempt. No one believed it was an accident and no one had the details right. They were all about the drama.

"Do you know when you're going to dance again?" Miss Tris asked.

"Jesus," Tayla snarled.

Tad pushed Miss Tris a little.

"It's okay," I said.

Dancing was my thing. Everyone knew I danced. Everyone wondered if I ever would again. Now that I couldn't, though, I saw things differently. Dancing lost a lot of its shine.

"Could be awhile," I said. "Week, the doctors said. Months maybe."

"You'll make it," Tad said.

I smiled a weak smile.

"You will," Tayla hissed at me. It seemed more important to her than me. All I could was nod. Tayla was in full-out fierce mode. I didn't want to fight.

"Okay," I said.

She stared at me until I looked away. I hated the way her face got when she was like this. I hated the thought of disappointing her. I hated the thought that if I didn't come back from this, she'd walk away.

Slipping

Midnight. One. Two. Three in the morning. I sat in a lawn chair on the patio listening to the planes growling through the sky. Next door, frogs filled the night with a throaty song. Mr. Rothgery's bathroom light flashed on. He was old. I imagined he peed a lot.

Lights from the city painted the clouds gray and yellow. The cigarette in my hand made menacing shadows.

Tayla came to the door. She came out and pressed her forehead to my spine, right between my shoulder blades.

"What're you doing?" she asked.

"It's too loud," I said.

She wrapped an arm around me, pressing her palm to my belly.

Nothing made sense. I heard rhythms in the frog song that weren't there. The planes in the air threatened to drop down and remove my head from my shoulders.

"Can I help?" Tayla asked.

I shook my head. Nothing helped. No one knew what to do. I was so confused.

Love

Oxy made everything okay. Not great. Just okay.

I stumped along the hall. Tayla carried my books. I got to my desk and sat. Across the room, Coy stared at me. Because I was high, it didn't matter. Tayla sat with me.

"You ready for this?" she asked.

I nodded. Mac came. He stopped at my deck and put his hand on my shoulder.

"You okay?" he asked.

I nodded.

"Good."

We talked about Chaucer. We talked about God and love. I was too stoned to follow. I floated, and the words washed through me, little bits of light and glass. I closed my eyes.

"Do you like this?" Gid asked in my head.

"What?"

"This," he said.

"What this?"

"This world," he said. "These walls. These people."

"They love me," I said.

He came, invisible, and kissed me. His lips were hot and sharp.

"I love you," he said.

"Really?"

"As long as you love me."

He went away. Tayla shook my shoulder. I blinked.

"Time to go," she said.

"Go?"

"Home," she said.

I nodded. Home. Bed. Away from here.

Lies

    I hurt. Every movement. Every breath. A grinding ache. I rose naked from bed. The cast was heavy and hard. The crutches wore sores in my pits and palms. I moved with a lurching stiffness. The bathroom down the hall seemed too far away but I made it. I sat and I peed and I thought of getting into the shower, using the water to pry the cast from my leg.
    I thought that I could kill myself now. I could take the rest of the oxy and fade away. I could open a vein and sit in a tub of hot water while the blood ran away. It was all clear in my head, vivid as a photo. I saw myself pale and blue in the shower, lying on the floor. I saw myself lying there waiting for Tayla to find me.
    But then I saw her face. I saw the confusion turn to shock then anger and grief. Killing myself would solve my problems. It would end this thing with Gid and the shit I took at school, but it would open wounds in people's lives that might never close. I couldn't do that. I couldn't spread pain like that. It was beyond unkind. It was cruel.

Things Come Out

"Sweet Jesus," Angie said. "You fuckered yourself up good."

She stood over the couch, too tall, too perfect. Tayla growled something. Angie waved a hand at her and sat.

"I was joking," she said. "Are you in pain?"

"Some," I said.

"I could get you something," she said. "The girls at the club…"

"She has pills," Tayla said.

"Okay," Angie said.

Her eyes rolled over me like a hand, somewhat slimy, too familiar. I knew her body. She knew mine.

"I just wanted to check on you," she said.

"Thanks."

Tayla turned to her piano, poking at the keys with depressed fingers.

"You have to be careful," Angie said. "You can't dance all busted up."

"I know."

She heard something. Tayla too.

"You okay?" Angie asked.

I nodded. It was a lie without lying. The thought of dancing was a mound of ash in my mouth.

"You'll be fine," Angie said.

It was a question without asking a question

"We'll see," I said.

She stared at me. She heard the words. Tayla too. They waited for more.

"We'll see," I said.

Silence filled with too many unsaid words filled the room.

"I'm tired," I said.

Angie nodded.

"Sure," she said.

She stood. Tayla stared at me. She knew things but what could she say? She took Angie to the door.

"See you soon," Angie said.

"Yeah," I said, the word blunt and hard as a hammer. Tayla flinched a little. When Angie was gone, Tayla didn't look at me. She took all the air out of the room and closed the door, leaving me choking on my secrets.

Fight

For days, we fought but we fought silently. We circled each other and pretended we had nothing to say. It was a long, wordless battle of sighs and swallowed snark. Meals were concentrated awkwardness. I sighed and Tayla glared and grumbled. Faces in the walls stared with eyes like boiled eggs. Moody, filmy flags floated and waved, unanchored and tattered.

I lie on the couch watching dust dance in the jaundiced light between me and the ceiling. Across the room, Tayla picked out a simple tune on her piano, one note at a time. Sound dripped onto the floor and rolled there, small and iridescent as mercury.

Suddenly, it stopped. Everything in the room went still. Me. Tayla. The notes in the air.

"You know," Tayla said, "all you ever wanted was to dance."

Something cold raced along my leg, aching deep in the bone. It wasn't a memory I wanted. I closed my eyes.

"I loved that in you," she said.

Words raced through me, jagged and hard. I wanted to explain. I wanted to shout and scream. Dancing was hard. Grace was hard. Rhythm and feeling were hard. It lost the touch. I lost the drive.

"It made you special," she said.

I didn't want to be special. I was used to living slowly now. My life was simple. I was big. Man big, but no one laughed at me for dreaming stupid dreams. Dancing was for limber, little girls. I was neither.

"Remember the things your mom used to say?" she asked.

This wasn't fair. Bringing my mom into things was mean. I couldn't even remember the last time I'd spoken to my mother. All my life, she had ridden me for being big.

"Butter," Mom used to say. "No one likes a weak character. If you tried," she'd say, "girls are supposed to be charming. If you want to be a dancer, you have to control yourself. Butter, people are going to think you're a lesbian."

When she found out Tayla and I were not just girlfriends but, *girlfriends* she lost her mind. She threatened and begged and when I wouldn't be the girl she wanted, she kicked me out.

"Do you remember how we met?" Tayla asked.

In the eighth grade, I stopped eating for a week. I sucked water down and I danced until my feet bled. That was how I met Tayla. She was in the band room banging out wild tunes and I was in the gym spinning and sweating. Her music punched into my spine and tossed me up. I couldn't stop. Voices told me to stop. Colors rolled through the room in streamers and misty walls. The floor felt too hard, too far away. I floated out of myself, but not completely. I was terrified. I was sick and weak and I spun too fast for too long. Everything went black. When things came back to me, Tayla held my head. I´d seen her before. She was the slightly Goth loudmouth. No one liked her. I avoided her because she said things no one wanted to hear and that scared me. I didn´t want to know what she thought of me. But just then, with my head in her lap, I couldn't stop staring.

"You ruined your feet," she said. "You couldn't walk for days."

"It hurts," I said.

"I know."

"All of the time," I said.

Again, she plinked the keys. Even with no direction or meaning, Tayla's music changed me.

"Everything hurts," I said.

She nodded.

"I'm done," I said.

She never looked at me. She turned away.

"Really?" she asked.

The word hung like a blade between us. Something cold and hard twisted in me. What could I say? This was more than just a talk. The was a ledge, tall and dangerous and beyond it nothing but a long fall.

"What do you want me from?" I asked.

She turned. Again, silence. Smoke and bone colored mist rose between us.

"I'm just remembering," she said.

But it was more than that. It was a warning. It was a shot, quiet and serious. She wanted me to come back to myself. I rolled onto my belly and closed my eyes; not sure I could do it.

Work Out

Each step was a marathon. Each breath a gasp. Even with the wind pounding me, I sweated. I walked and walked and Tayla walked with me, head down, red-faced. She muttered nasty words under her breath.

"We can go home," I said.

"No," she said. "Keep going." Tayla wasn't into exercise.

"Exercise," she said, "is for fat people and athletes and I am neither."

To Tayla pain was pain. It had no meaning or redeeming qualities. The only time she worked up a sweat was at the piano or in bed. But now, I needed to walk to get my legs back and Tayla needed to walk with me to make sure I made it home. She worried that I might step in front of a car again. She worried that I would die in a gutter somewhere.

I hauled my thick thighs down the road as fast as I could go. I would jog but jogging still hurt so I walked, and I walked until my legs quivered and my heart raced to the edge of my ribs.

"How long're we going to do this?" Tayla asked.

"Every day."

"Jesus."

At the corner, Tayla sat on the curb and rested her head on her knees.

"Are you okay?" I asked.

"Half dead," she said.

"Welcome to my world."

She gave me the finger and lay back on the sidewalk. People were starting to starc. We looked like a couple of sweaty old bag ladies. Standing over her I realized how much stronger I was. Being strong was good. Strength was important. Being strong was the only good thing about being so big.

An old man stopped. He looked from me to Tayla and back again. His beard, white and wispy, hung in thin strings from a wasted face. Ragged teeth in a thin mouth showed yellow and crusty.

"You okay?" he asked.

I stepped back. Something scared me. His hands waved at his sides, like a fish treading water. The smell of piss and beer rolled from him. I clenched my fists. I waited for the fight.

"I can call someone," he said, looking down at Tayla.

She opened her eyes and sat up.

"You okay, sweetheart?" the old man asked.

She looked from him to me and back again.

"Out of shape," she said, standing. "Let's go."

She got up, wobbly and weak but on her feet.

"Do you need a ride?" the old man said. "I have a car."

Tayla shook her head.

"We live close."

He smiled and walked away, stopping once and lifting a friendly hand.

"Home?" Tayla asked.

I nodded and started off, fast, with a purpose.

"Shit," Tayla said, jogging to keep up.

I tried to feel bad, but I couldn't. She wanted this. She would have to keep up.

First Try

"Dance for me," Tayla said.

She stroked her piano as if it were a kitten. Slow simple music. Gentle light filled the room like a mother's promise. I stood in the middle of the empty floor, filling my lungs with warm air.

"Dance for me," she said.

I didn't want to. I wanted to lie there and stare at the ceiling. I wanted to sleep. But Tayla's music coaxed a rhythm in me.

I moved cautiously, spinning on my good leg. Muscles bunched, out of practice. My arms rose like kelp in a tide. Tayla watched and played and I danced. I danced. I sweated. Heat rolled off of me, a nearly invisible wall of effort.

I didn't make it through the whole thing. Pain flashed from knee to hip. Black spots unfolded, grew and exploded in my eyes. I crumpled and cried. Tayla put her hands on my leg.

"What happened?"

"I'm dying."

"You're not dying," she said. "Everything will be fine."

But she couldn't know that. No one could. I needed to get out of here. I needed to get away from the pity, the failure. I hated myself. I needed to get away before things got really bad, before the world gave up on me all together.

Faith

There he was. Gid. In the window during Government, blotch of old blood. It was impossible. Government was on the second floor. I couldn't see the ground from my seat. All I saw were trees and the mountains on the horizon, eating the sky.

But there he was, standing just outside the window, watching me watch him. I tried to pretend that I didn't notice, but we both knew I did. Neither of us could ignore the other.

Mr. Hamlett stood at the front of the class talking about theocracies. He talked about Israel, the Vatican. He talked about Iran.

"When the state is married to a certain faith, any faith, it becomes an incestuous circle reinforcing the worst parts of dogma and doctrine."

Mr. Hamlett was a demagogue. He spread his propaganda like a gardener watering his plants. Not that he was wrong, but he never argued the other side. He seemed to think it was his calling to evangelize the Gospel of Atheism and Reason. Only there was very little of either in his class.

Gid lifted his hands and they were covered in blood.

"This is what I offer you," he said.

Anger roiled in my middle. Gid had no place here. I'd gotten used to life without him. I thought we were done but now, here he was, poking at me with his whispers.

Cold crystallized the bones in my hands. Tendons stretched. Muscles wept. Colored string pulled at every joint. My skin opened, and light seared every nerve.

"Pain," Gid said. "Turn away from the flesh."

Tears ran hot and hard.

"You're dying," Gid said.

I choked.

"They'll pull you apart," he said.

Suddenly, he was inside me, moving like melted glass. Mr. Hamlett called my name. I jerked and stared at him. Gid faded. Things settled.

"Do you think the Constitution offers freedom from religion as well as freedom of religion?" he asked.

I blinked.

"You think people, all people, all over the world should have the freedom to choose their own destiny?" he asked.

I swallowed.

"Are you with us?" I shook my head.

"Sorry," I said.

Mr. Hamlett frowned.

Gid touched the knobs of my spine with invisible fingers full of nothing but grief and blood.

The First Shot

Queertopia. Tayla, red-faced and clenched. Tad, pale and shaky. Miss Tris looked sick.

"What?" I asked.

"Fucking cowards," Tayla snarled.

I saw the crosses and the flyers and the pamphlets. I read through the front covers.

"Jesus," I said.

"No shit," Miss Tris said.

We gathered all of the pamphlets and flyers into a pile and ceremoniously dumped them into the garbage. Tayla got on the table and started shouting.

"You people think this is funny?" she screeched.

Everyone turned to her. They stopped talking. They stopped eating.

"You think we need your bible?" she demanded. "You think we need your God?"

Mr. Skarey came through the room and stood at the head of the table.

"Fucking pansies," Tayla said.

Mr. Skarey shook his head. He wasn't a bad guy, but sometimes he had to do some pretty shitty things.

"You can't stand on the tables, Tayla," he said.

"Whatever."

"Off the table," he said.

"Keep the bigots the fuck away from us then," Tayla said, jumping down.

"Language," Mr. Skarey said.

He stood there while we all settled into our seats and started in on our lunch. When we'd all turned our attention away from him, he wandered off.

"I'm going to kick Coy's ass," Tayla said.

"I don't know," I said.

"I have a plan," Miss Tris said. "Make those fuckers see us for real."

We'd need a stack of gay porn, several tubes of superglue and a bunch of dildoes. Her plan was a little out there, but it would definitely get us some attention.

Always and Forever

I dreamed of light and faceless faces. I dreamed of Gid's hands and the feel of his lips. I knew the ridges of his thighs and the swirls in his fingertips. His tongue tasted of mint and rain.

Scenes flipped from one to the other without warning. First, I was on a bus, trying to shave my head. I didn't know why I wanted to shave my head. I couldn't stop. I took a spoon and scraped it over my scalp over and over, but the hair wouldn't cut. It pulled at the roots, but nothing came off.

Gid sat with me, and stared, but I couldn't speak. Something told me he was smiling, like this was funny to him. Anger flooded through me. I bunched my fist, but then my body locked up and I couldn't do anything. I couldn't move. I couldn't breathe. I choked and gagged and shivered. Gid ran his fingertip along my jaw.

"This is love," he said. "You cannot get away."

The world tilted and spun, and I stood on a corner down by the water front. Rain fluttered in from the mountains. Men and women ran by me. I was invisible. Out on the river, tugs and ferries steamed through the red and silver waves. Water rose over the seawall and swirled around my ankles. I sank into the muddy bank. Trees reached out for me, but their fingers were too brittle, too weak.

I was dying.

"You can live forever," Gid said.

He stood on the water, not reaching for me, not doing anything to save me. I tried to climb his leg, but he was smoke and rain.

I slipped below the waves. Green light filtered in. I couldn't breathe. I kicked and fought, and my lungs quivered. Everything exploded.

I dreamed of music, but I didn't fly or float or dance. I stood in a room without walls, the floor hard and even, black as a broken promise. The sky was smooth, polished. A wind brushed my bones. Gid came out of the pearly air, blurred, solidifying after a moment of fear.

"Hush," he said.

Every piece of me quivered. The world changed. Gid lay with me on my bed. We kissed, and he swallowed me whole. His strong hands stroked me, cupped me, held me. Lips crawled down my belly to my thighs. I arced and screamed, and he plunged into me.

He pushed me into madness.

"Hush," he said.

His hands left a trail of sparks.

Temptation

Last call. The stage emptied and most of the girls were gone. Angie walked through the bar, rousting the drunks. The music stopped suddenly, and the room seemed naked without it.

Once all the drunks were gone, Benny locked the door and went back to the bar.

I mopped the floor, spinning around the handle, trying the beginnings of new moves. Angie stocked the bar. I cleaned the mirrors. She did the receipts.

"Ready?" she asked when we were done.

I stashed the buckets and shit in a closet off the dressing room.

"Let's get breakfast," she said.

I liked Angie. I didn't want to be awkward with her. But I was. Angie was all about flesh and fun. It made me nervous and excited and sometimes guilty because I knew her body as well as Tayla's. It was a dance thing. Rhythm and touch and sweat.

There was very little traffic on the street, so Angie pushed her little car as hard as she could. Streetlights blurred. Asphalt sparkled in the light from the headlamps like crystals thrown carelessly over black satin. I rolled down the window and lit a cigarette and watched for cops.

We zipped into the Pancake House's parking lot and Angie found a slot in the back.

"Can I ask you something?" Angie asked.

I shrugged.

"Do you like sex?" she asked.

"Jesus."

"What?"

"I don't know."

Angie flicked her filter out the window.

"This isn't — right, I guess," I said.

"Jesus," she said and got out.

A hostess took us to our table and we sat, neither of us talking, reading the menu. Now that we were here, I didn't feel like eating. My stomach was sour and twisted.

"Are you seeing someone?" I asked.

"There's a guy I see sometimes," she said.

"Okay," I said.

"It's not that way," she said.

She put her menu down and stared at me.

"Would you go home with me?"

All the light, all the air turned to amber. Angie smiled. She looked away and she looked back.

"So, this guy," she said.

"Yeah?"

"So, this guy," she said. "He's kind of rich."

Her smile was delicate and her eyes frail. Still, things were back to normal. Kind of. Not really.

Empty Promises

It started. But then it stopped. It started again. Things jerked around me like an old-fashioned film running too slowly. Everything spun. Fragments twisted in the pearly light. Faces formed. Large, ugly teeth gnawed at me. Every time I moved, the whole thing stopped and reset.

Gid came out of a field of wild iris and pressed himself against my back. I tried to scream but thorns tore my throat apart. My lungs cracked open. Cold split every bone. His bristling chin tore the skin on the back of my neck. When he kissed me between the shoulder blades, my spine splintered. My thighs tingled and cramped.

I reached for his eyes, clawing and digging.

"Show me," I said.

For a moment, he faded. His edges blurred but the light shifted, and the lines came back blade sharp. His fingers found my nipples and I yelped. We were naked, and I knew what was happening. Flesh fell from bone. My guts wrapped themselves around my spine. He pumped me full. My back arced. My toes curled.

Everything went white, then black.

I opened my eyes. I shook my head. I went to the bathroom and pissed. Blood stained the water. Was this my period? It wasn't time for my period.

"Fuck," I said. "Goddamn."

I turned away and found myself in the mirror. My face made no sense. It was only vaguely familiar like a photo of someone who looked a little like the picture I had of myself in my head but not quite. The skin was too pale. Darkness dug deep into the bones. Stony teeth worried at bloodless lips.

"Butter," Tayla called.

"I'm okay."

"What're you doing?"
"He was here."
"Butter," she said.
Even through the door she sounded angry.
"He was here!" I screamed.
"Okay," she said. "Okay."
"Okay," I whispered and opened the door.
"What's wrong?" Tayla asked.
"It doesn´t make sense," I said.

She reached out and I flinched and flinched again when she snapped her hand back to her side. With everything running through me, a touch, no matter how soft or well meaning, could kill.

"Sorry," I said.
She nodded.
"Come back to bed," she said.
She turned away. I followed, hating every step, hating the thought of lying down again where Gid could find me.

Gifts

Music rose into the air, bright and clean. Cigarette smoke haloed the stage light. Spinning sparks danced through the air. Candles burned on every table. I sat up front watching Tayla's magic up close, watching people fall in love with her.

Time vanished. The world failed to spin. Nothing mattered but the amber music.

But then it ended.

When the last note sang out into the darkness, silence fell for a long moment before everyone stood and yelled. Tayla sat at the piano, bowed over the keys for a long time. Worry ate at me, but then she stood. The last of the amber music evaporated. Even from here, I could tell she was exhausted. She looked ready to cry. I climbed the stage and wrapped her in my arms. I kissed her nose. I kissed her ear. She leaned into me. I held her, and she sighed.

"Jesus," she said.

People wandered around and talked. Iridescent scraps played around them.

"Can we sit somewhere?"

I looked around. There were so many people. There were so many ways things could wrong. I swallowed. Tayla looked at me. I swallowed again, and I nodded.

"Really?" she asked.

She kissed me. I looked around. No Gid. No danger. Still I looked and Tayla saw me looking.

"You sure?" she asked.

I kissed her. She grinned.

"I'm right here," she said.

I squeezed her hand. She winced. She smiled. We walked into the crowd.

The Plan Comes Together

We gathered in the Shack for a cigarette an hour before the sun rose. Darkness hung on the trees like dark robes. Light from the school was dim and distant. Our faces were all black and red from our smokes. No one said anything. At our feet sat bags, one of cut-up porn, gay porn, men fucking men and women fucking women, one filled with jumbled dildos. We each had two tubes of super glue.

Out front, the parking lot was empty. Every so often, a car pulled in and dropped the kids for zero-hour jazz band. The front door was unlocked. We finished our cigarettes and lifted our supplies and went to work.

The halls were a little creepy without the noise of students going from class to class, hanging out at their lockers talking and laughing, shouting and throwing things at each other. Only every third light burned. Soft shadows lay on the walls. We walked to the cafeteria. The room was empty. Not even the food people were there yet.

Moving quickly, we got to work. We glued the porn to the table tops. We taped three or four photos to a table. On the seats, we glued the dildos, sticking up like dick-shaped thorns. Whenever a noise leaked in from the hallway, we froze. Not that we thought we'd get away with it, but the rabbit part of us wouldn't shut off.

Once everything was set, we went to Queertopia and hung a banner we'd made. It read:

It's not a lifestyle. It's an eating disorder.

After that we stood in the center of the room and looked around, wondering in the glory of mischief and revenge. This would teach them to taunt us with their scriptures and fears.

"The gay agenda strikes back," I said.

Tayla laughed and kissed me. No matter what happened next, for a moment, everyone would know our names.

Object of Admiration

Mr. Skarey called us all into his office and we all waited for our turn. We all knew what this was about. This was about the porn and the dildos in the cafeteria. The waves rattled through the school for weeks. Parents called and came in. Parents bitched and threatened. Mr. Skarey had to do something, so he called the most likely suspects.

Everyone knew it was us. Coy stopped us in the hall.

"I suppose you thought it was funny," he said.

"It was hil-fucking-larious," Tayla said.

"You people are disgusting," Coy said.

We walked away and now we were in the office waiting a chance to tell our story.

Mr. Skarey called me in. I sat in the chair near the door.

"So," Mr. Skarey said, "what can you tell me?"

I stared at him.

"We both know it was you guys," he said. "No one else…"

"Everyone else just plasters our table with hate mail," I said. "They leave nasty notes in my locker."

"That doesn't warrant…"

"What?" I asked. "Responding in kind?"

"So, you admit…"

"I admit nothing," I said.

"What am I supposed to do?" he asked.

"Nothing."

"Nothing?"

"You can't stop this."

Somehow, Mr. Skarey's eyes got tired and duller.

"Tell folks to mind their own business," I said. "And then maybe we can get along."

"Is that what you want?" he asked.

"No," I said. "I want a pony."

Freak Out

I went to bed at three. I got up at six. I went back to bed at eleven. I was up at two. I rested on the couch but couldn't relax. Minutes and hours passed. I finished one cigarette and started another.

Four days vanished with no sleep and I saw things. Dark men followed me. I couldn't eat. The food was poisoned. There were people in the world trying to kill me. They thought my dances were code to the CIA. They thought I was a spy. But I wasn't. I wasn't a spy. I was just a fat girl, a dancer, a student. Faces came at me out of the light, feral and famished. Gid circled like a bat in a wounded sky.

"Stay away," I said.

"Butter."

Tayla stood in the doorway, too far off to help. Her voice was an echo in the corners.

Clothes scraped at me so I got naked. Cold air scrubbed the sweat from my skin and hair, leaving the salt, a thin, grainy layer.

"I love you," Gid said.

"Fuck you," I said. "Go away."

Tayla came with heavy hands and a tear-scarred face.

"Who're you talking to?" Tayla asked.

Words failed me. I flung around. She spun with me, looking, trying to see. She couldn´t.

"She's blind," Gid said. "She doesn't see what you see."

"I will kill you!"

I lunged. Gid was there and not there. Glass broke.

"Jesus!"

Tayla grabbed me and pulled me to the floor. Blood flowed. Tendons rolled and pulled. White flesh and red muscle bunched. I kicked and slammed my head on the floor. Glass planted itself in my back.

"Stop," Tayla begged. "Please stop."

Black birds came from the corners.

"This," Gid said, "lasts forever."

But then he left, taking the menace with him.

"Are you okay?" Tayla asked.

I nodded and swallowed. I was done. I was empty, cored out.

"Really?" she asked.

I tucked my head into her lap and closed my eyes. She stroked my hair. She cried, and I tried to feel something, but there was nothing there. Not even guilt for not feeling guilty.

Vows and Promises

Tayla's hair was a perfect mess, not tangled, but wild all the same, sticking up at angles. Her fingers skimmed over the keys. Notes, light as a mother's prayer, filled the room. Everything in room sparkled. Something in me lifted and twisted in the room's corners up near the ceiling. For the first time, nothing mattered. A weird hope eased along my body's edges.

Tayla played without thought or worry. Somehow, she was both concentrated and diluted. She was immortal, sitting in the blue and red lights covering the stage. She was absolutely beautiful.

Without thought or purpose I moved from the couch. I ran my hands up under her shirt to her nipples. I kissed the back of her neck. She turned, and she ran her fingers through my hair. She kissed me.

"What was that for?" she asked.

"I felt like it."

I abandoned caution and safety. Tayla squealed and twitched when I lifted her from her bench. Because I was big, she was nothing more than a warm pressure against my chest.

"What're you doing?" she asked.

"Hush," I said.

She curled into me and kissed the muscles along my throat. She kissed my chin's tip.

"I love you," she said.

"I know."

"Good."

We spoke without words. Our hands made their own language, a language of sweat and lips and sighs, a language no one spoke but Tayla and me. It was a promise and a vow. It was a prayer and a sacrifice.

This Body

    I dreamed of music, complicated, syncopated, rhythmic music. Drums rattled my bones. Guitars wailed like angry children. Fiddles screamed over the top, turning the whole thing white and red. I didn't fly or float. I danced. The room was hard and even. Everything was smooth, polished. A wind brushed my bones.

    This wasn't my body. This body was too thin, too strong. I twirled and soaked in the shadowless light. I was weightless, and I couldn't stop. I was in my body but out of it too. It was as if I were a marionette, dangling from frayed strings. I tried to stop over and over. I couldn't. Panic and nausea flooded through me. Anger and fear turned me to a knife blade. I cut through the air and the light. I told myself over and over that I was dreaming. I told myself I could wake anytime. But I couldn't. I couldn't wake.

    Gid came out of the translucent air, blurred, then livid before solidifying. Every piece of me quivered. He lifted me and threw me into the sun. My skin crisped and my hair crackled.

    No one had ever lifted me. I was too strong, too big. But Gid was bigger and stronger. His hands scarred my flesh. I screamed and screamed, and he laughed. He kissed the back of my neck, his lips lines of flames.

    "Please," I said.

    I hated the sound of my voice. It was whiney and thin. Everything was weak and sour.

    The walls closed in and the light changed. My arms and legs crackled and bent. Something sharp pushed into my belly. Gid swallowed me whole.

    "This is love," he said.

    I reached for his face, but it was dark and all I saw were cheekbones, the bridge of his nose.

    "Don't," he said.

He turned to smoke and mist and rose into the empty space above us. He was gone. Music rushed in with sunlight and the feeling that things were going to get bad.

Miracles

    I was late. I was never late. Since I was thirteen years old, I bled every twenty-eight days. It was the same every month. It was a weird kind of relief.

    Now, though, now, I was late, and I didn't know what was happening.

    I had two tests. They came in blue boxes with blue and white sticks wrapped in plastic. I pissed on one. I pissed on one and I waited. Mom and Tayla were downstairs making coffee and eggs. They were frying eggs and toasting bread. I couldn't stand the thought of eating. I felt sick.

    Morning sickness? Nerves? Fear?

    I pissed on the stick and I waited and when the waiting was done, a little blue cross hung in the little window. I was pregnant. I couldn't be pregnant. I was a dyke and dykes didn't get pregnant. Not on accident. For dykes, babies were planned.

    I pissed on the other stick and it too came up blue. My belly turned, and I puked in the sink. Fuck! Jesus! What was I going to do? This wasn't part of the plan. This couldn't be happening. Dreams and ghosts didn't knock girls up. It wasn't possible. None of this made sense. I stared at the test until Tayla tapped on the door.

    "What're you doing?" she called.

    "I'm okay," I said.

    "We're going to be late," she said.

    I smiled a bitter smile. She had no idea.

Thoughts

Biology was a class of long tables and windows that would not open. Class was all about mitosis and cell division and all I could think about were the cells in my belly dividing and growing into a baby. I had no idea what I was going to do. I had to tell Tayla. But I had no idea what I would say. I mean, it wasn't like to buy the whole virgin birth thing.

Somehow, I felt empty. Muted colors echoed in my body. Thoughts and scenarios spun through me. I saw myself sleeping in an alley with the baby curled against me. I saw myself dancing in Angie's club for tips. I saw myself working a corner, selling sex bit by bit. Suicidal fantasies invaded me like ants crowding around crumbs of stale bread. It would be so easy to just do what the voices told me to do. I could float into oblivion in water pinked with blood from slit wrists. Things would be so much easier, better maybe, if I were dead. No one would hate me. I wouldn't hate myself.

"Do it," the voices said.

"I'll be there," Gid said.

Tears burned my face's soft flesh. The thoughts swirled and crashed against one another, breaking into jagged fragments. They scraped me raw.

For an hour, I stared at nothing. Words and sound ricocheted from me. I was a pillar of stone. Nothing meant anything. All I wanted was for everything to stop. I needed time and room to breathe but I had neither.

"This is a gift," Gid said.

His invisible hand stroked my belly.

"We did this," he said. "This is real. This is love."

I pushed him away. His voice turned to light and dimmed. His hands faded.

When the bell rang I shuffled with everyone else out to the hall. Kids swirled around one another, talking, griping and laughing. I had nothing to laugh about. I felt sick. The bathroom down the hall smelled of Lysol and bleach. Girls washed their hands and did their makeup and I wanted nothing to do with them. I was going to puke, but puking with everyone there watching and listening was not good. People would talk. People made monsters from nothing. Stories would float through the school like jellyfish going with the current. I would never hear the end of it. It would get back to Tayla and I'd have to tell her something. I hated lying but I hated the thought of losing her more.

    In a stall, the porcelain toilet was cold against my thighs and I sucked the antiseptic air into my lungs and waited. When the last bell rang and the bathroom emptied, I allowed myself to puke. Spasms wracked my middle. Nothing came up but bile. It was not fun but when it was done, I felt a little better.

    I washed my face and rinsed my mouth. I stared for a moment at the mirror. Water slicked my round cheeks. My thick jaw and soft chin bothered me. I turned away and left. I went to my locker. I sat on the floor, back against the thin metal. All I wanted was to go home. All I wanted was for my life to slide back into place. This was the end of the world as I knew it. These were the last breaths I would breathe as a real person.

No God

Religion and government. Faith and rules. A Christian group wanted to start a prayer club. Mr. Hamlett fought it.

"The first amendment gives us freedom from religion," he said in class. His face was narrow and his teeth crooked. He ranted for half the class. "I learned in Vietnam," he said, "there was no God."

None of us said anything. Mr. Hamlett taught from the top down. He said what he wanted, and we listened. None of us took notes. There was nothing so important that we needed to remind ourselves.

"The idea of Jesus is good," he said, "but the dogma and doctrine have spoiled the message."

Sunlight turned the room gold and warm. It was one of those cruel spring days where the world looked bright and balmy. People dressed in shorts and tees. They went outside, and the cold mountain winds cut straight through their flesh.

"I am a God-fearing man," Mr. Hamlett said. "I fear that if there is a God, He's determined to punish us into oblivion."

Coy raised his hand. Mr. Hamlett refused to see it for a moment.

"I have a question," Coy said.
Mr. Hamlett sighed.
"Mr. Henderson," he said.
"Do you believe in love?" Coy asked.
"Mr. Henderson," Mr. Hamlett said.
"No," Coy said. "Really."
Sucking in air, Mr. Hamlett nodded.
"Yes," he said. "I believe in love."
"How can there be love without God?" Coy asked.
"Mr. Henderson," Mr. Hamlett said, "this is not a religion class."

"You're talking religion," Coy said.

"I'm talking about philosophy and government."

"This country was founded to be a Christian country," Coy said. "You have to accept that."

Mr. Hamlett's face turned a fierce florid color like sweet peas or old blood.

"Without God," Coy said, "there is no love."

"Love," Mr. Hamlett said, "is a human trait."

"So is God," Coy said.

Mr. Hamlett's teeth squealed against each other. Murmurs floated like fluff through the room.

"If you love God," Coy said, "he loves you."

"Your God is hateful at best," Mr. Hamlett said.

"God only hates sinners," Coy said.

"Where does your God get off telling us what is sin, and what is virtue?" Mr. Hamlett demanded.

"He's God," Coy said. "He makes the rules."

"Not in my classroom," Mr. Hamlett said.

Almost

Breakfast came at me in waves. Grease sputtered and popped in the skillet. Smoke rose in oily strands. Eggs bubbled, turning white and solid. Bread toasted. It was too much. All the smells hit me like gusts of heavy wind. My gut danced. I sucked in shallow breaths.

"Tell her," Gid said.

He sat with me at the table. His strong wine-colored hands splayed on the cheap wood in front of him.

"This is your fault," I said.

Tayla turned to me.

"What?" she asked.

"Nothing."

She narrowed her eyes.

"Really," I said.

Gid sat back against the chair. Somehow, Tayla didn't hear the floor creak or the sigh he sighed.

"This is not going away," he said.

"Hush," I said.

From the corner of my eye, I saw Tayla tense. It was time to go. I went out for a cigarette. Gid met me on the patio. Gray rain tried to wash him away and failed.

"You need to stop," I said.

He came with hard, hot hands and grabbed my belly.

"Is this real enough?" he asked.

I jerked away.

"Go away," I said. "Jesus. Just go."

"You know better than that," he said.

Tayla came to the door.

"Breakfast," she said.

I nodded and came in. Gid apparently decided he'd said enough. I sat at the table with Tayla, neither of us willing to talk about the obvious. It was awkward and unpleasant.

Tayla's drawn face tore at me.

"Hey," I said.

"Yeah?"

I nearly did it then. I nearly let the words slip through my teeth. But then Gid's voice echoed into me.

"She's going to leave," he said.

"I love you," I said.

Tayla stared for a moment. Questions formed in her eyes and died there. Part of me broke.

"Okay," Tayla said.

But we both knew it wasn't.

Help

Steam rolled up and broke against the ceiling. The fan chopped the air to ribbons. I sat in the tub with the hot, hot water pounding on my head. I heaved and hurled. I shuddered and gagged until my belly felt as if it were turning inside out.

Tayla knocked. She needed to pee. I swallowed bile and ash. Tayla came in.

"You okay?" she asked.

"Fine."

She peed and stuck her head through the curtain. Her eyes were dark.

"What's going on?" she asked.

I shook my head. Words gathered in my throat like ground glass. I wanted to tell her. I wanted to tell her about the baby. I couldn't. She thought Gid was just a figment, a shard of my imagination.

None of this was real to her. How could I convince her that some dreams were real? How could I convince her I'd done nothing wrong?

She went away, and the water turned cold. Moving with care and grace, I dried and dressed. I stepped into the bedroom barefoot and wobbly. Tayla waited. She was the center holding me together. Without her, I'd float away into misty madness. Everything would spin away. I'd have nothing but voices and false faces. I'd have nothing but Gid.

"You look worried," she said.

I nodded.

"Want to talk about it?" she asked.

"Nothing to say."

She frowned. She touched my chin and kissed my lips.

"I can help," she said.

"Not now," I said. "Nothing can help now."

This Is Love

First, I saw his hands. My body knew Gid's hands. They knew every crease, every callus. They knew the swirl of every finger. I knew the lines of his palms like scripture. They reached for me, glowing sharp and sapphire. I jerked away and slapped them down.

"I'm done," I said.

He came out of the shadows, his face still blurred and foreign.

"Show me," I said.

He stepped back.

"I need to know," I said.

His chest swelled. The muscles flexed. His belly was a bowl of shadow leading down to a crotch I didn't want to think about.

"That's not how it works," he said.

I turned away.

"My face is my secret," he said.

I walked a few steps.

"This is all there is," he said.

I spun, sharp and hard. The heel of my hands drove into his ribs. A grunt. A step back. Black rage roared through me.

"I swear to God," I snarled.

The light around him flickered before flaring. He charged me.

"This is love," he said.

"No!"

"This is reality," he said.

He clamped my wrists with a vicious grip. Bones ground and groaned. Pain shot to the center of my belly.

"You cannot live without me," he said. "People like you need people like me."

Animal noises ripped out my throat. Spinning and kicking, I went beast crazy. He held tight, so I rushed in and bit his neck. Features formed for a moment on his face. A flash of a nose, sharp and regal. A sliver of a chin, fox narrow. One eye, startled and wide, blinked for a moment.

"I do not!" I howled. "I do not! I do not! I do not!"

Slowly, calm came back. Air filled my lungs. My belly twisted with regret and the need to feel no regret.

"I'm dying," I said.

"Yes."

"I don't want to die."

"No one wants to die," he said.

I found a corner and sunk into it. The room spun around me.

"This is what life is," Gid said. "Want and pain and then death."

"Jesus."

He went away. I still wanted to hit things. I wanted to break the world into manageable pieces and chew them up. I wanted to swallow the light and live forever.

Making Sure

    Posters of smiling women and children broke the walls up into pale blocks. Magazines filled with stories about families lay on the coffee tables. An old woman sat at the receptionist table and asked my name.
    "Butter," I said, and she checked her computer.
    A woman with a baby sat in the corner looking too poor to support a child. Some kind of light music played, just barely loud enough to hear.
    "The doctor will be with you soon," the old woman said.
    I sat on the loveseat and waited. I wanted a cigarette. I wanted to pretend this wasn't happening. Voices whispered at me. I couldn't make out words, but the sound ate my nerves. I waited and watched the faces in the posters writhe and wrinkle. This was not a good day.
    Part of me wanted Tayla to be here. Part of me was glad she wasn't. I had to get through this. I had to know what the next step was before talking to her.
    They called me back. The hall was short. The walls were too pale. Open doors showed rooms with exam tables and clean tile counters. My room was at the end. The nurse took my vitals and chatted about something. I couldn't concentrate.
    After she left, I lay on the exam table and drew lines from one point on the ceiling to another. I waited, and I felt sick. My head buzzed, and the room seemed to twist on itself. Minutes passed. I came close to leaving, but then the doctor came.
    "My name's Angel," she said.
    "Butter."
    "What can I do for you?"
    I told her about the baby but not about Gid. I told her I was scared and didn't know what to do. She never blinked. She never frowned. She gave me a list of options. I could abort. I could put

the baby up for adoption. We talked about the meds I took, and she made notes.

"If you're going to keep the baby," she said, "you'll need to go off your meds."

Off my meds? I didn't like the thought of that. Things got wild when I was off my meds. I couldn't sleep. Visions and voices filled my world. But I couldn't really think of killing the baby. I wasn't much into spiritual things but the thought of cutting the baby out of my belly turned me sick.

The doctor gave me vitamins and nausea meds. She said she could help me through the pregnancy. She asked if the father was part of my life.

"I don't know," I said. "He doesn't know."

"Sooner's better than later," she said.

I thought about that. Maybe she was right, but what could I say? How was I going to convince Tayla I hadn't turned on her?

Something Hard and Sad

Rain fell like sand from a sky filled with clouds the color of raw wool. Rain cut through the petals of the blossoming cherry trees growing along the road. I stood in the Shack with Miss Tris smoking a cigarette. I felt like shit. My belly hurt. My tongue tasted of bile and ash.

"We're getting married," Miss Tris said.

"You and Tad?"

"I'll be eighteen in three months," she said. "Tad'll be eighteen in five. We're thinking of doing it on his birthday."

"What about your folks?" I asked.

Something hard and sad crossed her face. Shit. Miss Tris had an on again, off again thing with her folks. She was the youngest and when she was born, she was the only son of an only son. Her folks were good with the whole Trans thing, but her dad mourned the end of his line. Miss Tris would never have a son. There would be no Michael Hale the fourth.

"Dad's cool," Miss Tris said. "Mom's thrilled."

She stared up at the ceiling, through a crack there letting in dribbles of water.

"I just wish," she said, her voice distant, "you know, it would be easier if I were born right."

"At least you have Tad," I said.

Tayla and I sometimes talked about getting married, but Tayla wasn't all for it.

"Marriage," she said, "is a het thing. I don't do het things."

Something got sharp. Miss Tris looked at me.

"You okay?" she asked.

She was my best friend. But she was Tayla's best friend too. What I said here would be said to Tayla. So, I just shrugged.

"You know Tayla," I said. "All rebellion and fight."

Miss Tris didn't buy all of it, but she bought enough. She let it rest.

"Are you and Tayla doing Prom?" Miss Tris asked, out of nowhere.

I smiled and shook my head. Prom was a het thing too. Along with romance and babies.

"You know," I said, "after Homecoming."

She nodded.

"Yeah," she said. "Homecoming. No Bueno."

Miss Tris smiled. She knew the real story. The real story was Tayla thought refusing to be part of the world as it existed was for pansies. Tayla had to put a pin in anything that reeked of normal.

"You should see my dress," Miss Tris said, changing the subject. "It's the color of love."

The color of love? Jesus. What color was that? Was it the color of Tayla's eyes or the line of her lips when she smiled? Maybe it was the color of the water in the toilet after I puked all night. Maybe it was the color of Tayla's face when she found out I was pregnant.

Looking Forward

Dance Team girls gathered around Jessica Barber, shoulder to shoulder. Sometimes one pushed into another. Everyone wanted to be close. Jessica sat in the cafeteria with her daughter. The baby was tiny and smooth. A pink blanket wrapped the girl tight. I wondered how she could breathe.

"Fucking ridiculous," Tayla said.

Jessica looked tired. Still, her hair was done up right. Her jeans fit her perfectly. Her teeth were too white in a mouth painted too red. Eye shadows hid a darkness.

"Can you believe this shit?" Tayla asked.

We sat in Queertopia. The room was mostly empty at the end of the day.

"Who brings a baby to school?" Tayla asked. "Fucking hypocrites."

Most of the girls there were part of the chastity club. They walked around looking all superior and moral because they took a pledge they couldn´t keep. And none of them saw the sadness in what was happening. All they saw was a doll. All they saw was the romance of the thing.

"She says she didn´t know," Tayla said. "Bullshit."

Gid came and sat with us. I wouldn´t look at him.

"This," he said, "is you."

Soon, even the teachers came to Jessica's table. Mr. Skarey carried a smile like a blade. He didn't reach or coo like the Dance Team girls, but he was part of it. All he saw was the joy and momentary mania.

"Her life is over," Gid said. "Yours too."

I sighed. Tayla turned to me. Bitterness and anger pulled the skin around her eyes tight. It was not a pleasant look.

"She'll never believe you," Gid said.

"Stop," I said.

Tayla looked at me.

"Why?"

"Never mind," I said.

"All of this," Gid said, "is illusion."

Across the room, Jessica stood with the baby in her arms. The Dance Team girls swirled around her like dust in a wind.

"I have to feed her," Jessica said.

"Jesus," Tayla said. "Come on."

She pulled at my hand.

"This is so fucked," she said.

I couldn't move.

"Tell her," Gid said. "End it."

I couldn't. The words were too heavy. They sat in my belly with the baby, growing bit by bit, a light hazing the lines of everything in my life.

Closet

Water stains made dark masks on the cinder block walls. Fluorescents flickered under old tiles. I stood in the corner counting the holes in the ceiling. Someone told me once, if you hit yourself hard enough, you can knock a baby right out of your belly.

No one knew I was here. No one ever came here. Mops and buckets stood around waiting for someone to put them to work. Old ducts ran rusted in the corners. I didn't really know what I was going to do, but I knew I was going to do something.

I lay on the floor and lifted a spare cinder block over my chest. It was too heavy, too sharp at the corners. I benched it. One. Two. Three times. I benched and then tossed it at the ceiling. It went up and it came down. Right on my belly, crushing the wind out of me, pushing lunch back up to my mouth. Pain shot clean through me. My kidneys jumped, and my innards danced. I curled and cried.

When I could swallow a mouthful of air, I checked my middle. Scrapes and bruises, small bloody beads. It hurt, but it didn't hurt the way I thought it should. I was hoping for something deep, something substantial, not this tearing, electric shock. Over and over, I lifted and dropped the brick myself. Blood and sweat mixed. My hands and arms got weak. They trembled, and I had to stop.

Aching and sad, I washed my hands in the big metal sink. The water hissed, and bit and I chewed my lip. I scrubbed the blood from my belly and started building the lie I would tell Tayla. I fell, I'd say. I tripped and sprawled in the street. It was a weak lie but plausible. Tayla might suspect something but suspecting was not knowing.

Fine

"You're getting fatter," Coy said.

Wet lips writhed in his wormy face. I ignored him. He followed me down the hall. People watched. No one said anything. They were witnesses, silent and useless, there for the show. To them, this was entertainment.

"Did you eat Tayla this morning?" Coy asked. "Wait! Of course, you did!"

People snickered. Coy's eyes scanned the audience for support. Not much but enough to push him forward.

"Cannibalism's bad for you," he said.

I curled my shoulders and pushed through the crowd. No one tried to stop me.

"Gluttony's a sin," Coy called.

Giggles tumbled against the walls. I got to class but the door was locked. I was trapped.

"I'm not going away," Coy said.

"Gadfly," I said. "Just a gadfly."

"What?" Coy asked.

He got in my face. Even knowing that I'd kicked his ass in the past, Coy was courageous. Stupid but courageous.

"Nothing," I said.

His eyes watered and wandered around in his head.

"You're high," I said.

"You're ugly," he snapped. "At least I'll sober up."

"Yes," I said. "But I got laid this morning. When was the last time someone other than your momma touched your dick?"

Gasps and laughter. Coy blinked and thought. His mouth worked. He swallowed.

"Fuck you," he snapped and walked away.

My knees wobbled. I wanted to puke. Someone smacked my shoulder and said something nice. Mac opened the door to class. I stumbled.

"You okay?" he asked.

"Fine," I said and found my desk. Fucked up. Insecure. Neurotic. Emotional. Fine. Everything was fine.

Faces

Faces melted. Jaw lines narrowed and stretched. Teeth grew pointed and yellow. Eyes dropped into dark wells and foreheads grew into bony, ridged Neanderthal domes. I stood in the hall and watched, and the faces watched me. I stood in the hall waiting for someone, something to come out of the dusty light to eat my heart. Jaundiced strips waved in tatters, like bits of flesh pulled free of bone.

When the bell rang, it rang forever. Walls buzzed, and doors slammed. I was alone. I stood, frozen, scared, locked in place. I could not run or hide. These monsters knew how to hunt me.

Mr. Skarey found me. He said something, my name maybe, a spell to tear out my throat. He came, and he put his face into mine. He smelled of coffee and donuts. His eyes rolled free of each other. This was it. I was dying.

"Are you okay?" he asked.
Somehow the words slithered through the panic. His words made sense but still all I could do was shudder. When he put his hand on my shoulder I screamed, and he jumped, and we circled each other, feral and fierce.

Things changed again. The voices told me to hide. The voices told me to get out of the building. I felt sick. I tried to run, but Mr. Skarey was faster than me.

"Stop," he said. "Just stop. Please."
I found a window. It refused to open. It refused to move out of my way. A chair waited for me in the corner and I swung like a stick at Mr. Skarey. I swung it like a weapon at the window. These were super windows. They did not break. They just rattled and stood between me and life. I swung and swung and swung and then someone took me down. Someone grabbed my wrists and sat on my back.

"The baby! Jesus, the baby!"

Somehow it stopped. Somehow the racket dimmed, and the faces settled back to human standard. People gathered around to watch. Some of them looked scared. Others looked amused. A few people recorded the whole thing. It would be online soon. Shame and disgust soured everything.

Mr. Skarey asked if I was okay. I choked a little on the words, but they eventually fell out.

"Fine," I said. "I need to go home. I'm sick."

Mr. Skarey pulled me to my feet. He walked me away from the people watching. We got to a corner and stopped.

"Can you tell me about the baby?" Mr. Skarey asked.

"What baby?"

"You screamed about a baby," he said.

"There's no baby."

"Is there something I should know?"

"There's always something everyone should know."

Mr. Skarey made a face. I'd seen it before. It was his *you're not playing nice* face. I didn't really care. I wasn't going to play by his rules just because he felt bad.

The Beginning of the End

The bar was closed and empty. It was quiet and dark and warm as a wish. None of the little lamps on the tables burned. Neon signs turned the walls blue and red and green. Track lights glowed in strips on the ceiling.

Angie paid me a hundred bucks to clean the place three times a week. I stacked chairs and pushed a heavy mop around the room. Little steps. Music in my head. It was a narrow little dance. I washed glasses and wiped things down. All in all, it took two hours. Two hours of quiet and time alone.

Angie worked in her office, doing receipts and all the paperwork that kept the place running. Sometimes Tayla came with me, but tonight, tonight I was alone. Kind of.

Gid came and went like a bruise. He hid in the bathroom, sometimes the storage room. He whispered promises, but it didn't matter. I wasn't talking to him. I had things on my mind and they were none of his business.

"You can't ignore me forever," he said.

I turned away.

"Everywhere you go," he said, "I'll be there."

My hands gripped the mop handle too tight. My knuckles popped, and my fingertips turned white.

"We're tied together," he said. "Forever."

I spun too fast and slipped a little on the wet floor. I didn't fall but I looked ridiculous.

"Show me," I snarled.

He backed away.

"Do it," I said. "Your face. Show me."

He held up his hands.

"What're you afraid of?" I asked. "If you're real, if any of this means shit, show me. Show me! Goddammit it! Show me."

Something shifted. I saw an eye. I saw a forehead's dome. I saw him fade a little. I stopped.

"I love you," Gid said.

He went away. I was alone.

Slowly, the draining rage leaving me weak, I stumbled to the bar. I poured some vodka and sat on a stool sipping it, telling myself one drink wouldn't hurt the baby. When Angie came out of the office I stood. Even now, at the end of the night, she was all sex and heat. She stopped with her eyes stuck to my face.

"You okay?" she asked.

"Sure."

Something told me that she didn't believe me, but she said nothing.

"Ready?" she asked.

I nodded. It was a lie though. I was never going to be ready. I was never going to be ready again.

Kind of a Moment

I had a plan. For the plan to work, I had to talk to Coy. Alone.

The thought of talking to Coy made me a little sick. Every time we'd spoken, he ran me down. He made fun of me. He tore at me. I hated the idea of being alone with him. But it had to happen. I had a plan.

Coy and I had only two classes together, but I knew he always went to the bathroom during sixth period to get high. I had journalism. Halfway through, I went out to the hall. The hall was empty. Voices echoed from the hard, blue walls, some of them whispered from the classrooms, teachers lecturing or arguing with students. Some of the voices echoed only in my head.

Coy used the bathroom on the second floor in the Science Wing. I waited for him outside the bathroom. I hid behind some lockers and waited and then he came. We were the only ones here. I watched him slip silently into the john and waited for a minute. I waited because I wasn't sure the plan would work. I waited because I wasn't sure what I was going to say. I waited, because this was scary.

When I got the guts to go in, I went in hard. I slammed the door open hard enough for the sound of it to ricochet from the tiles. Coy sat in a stall. The skunky smell of weed hung like a stain in the air.

"We need to talk," I said.

Coy peeked out.

"You and me," I said.

His face folded a little, his lips frowning. Small lines crinkled the skin between his brows.

"What the hell?"

"I need your help," I said.

He banged the stall door closed.

"You're not a guy," he said. "No matter what you think."

I almost walked out. Asking Coy for anything, much less help, was not something I wanted to do, but there was no one else to ask.

"I need you to kill me," I said.

"What?"

"I'm pregnant."

A moment of silence but then he started laughing.

"I thought you…dykes don't get pregnant."

"I need you to kill me," I said.

"You're crazy."

"Will you do it?"

"Why not just do it yourself?"

"I can't."

He thought for a moment. He thought for a moment and then he came out and leaned on one of the sinks. His face was too narrow and too pale, and I could see everything going on in his head.

"You fucked a guy?" he asked.

"I don't want to talk about it."

"You fucked a guy," he said, "and now you want me to kill you."

"Go to hell."

I turned to go.

"I could take you to the doctor," he said.

I didn't know what to do. I didn't know what to say.

"My mom had an abortion last year," he said.

"Your mom?"

"I know this place…"

"No."

For a second, he became human. For a second, he stopped being the slimy little shit he was.

"I can't kill you," he said.

"Fine."

When I got to the door, he said my name.

"It'll be okay," he said.

Shaking my head, I went back to the hall and back to class. I sat in my chair thinking maybe the world really was ending. I was pregnant with a child whose father wasn't real and Coy Henderson, the school shit, was kind for moment.

Heavy

Music and movement. I spun and rose out of myself. Lights from the corners played over me like fingers. Shadows, hard edged and black, whirled with me. The music was all drums, banging and clanging, rubbing against me like a wind. I closed my eyes.

Not a good idea.

The room swirled like water in a toilet. Color bent and wrapped around my head. Faces formed and snapped at me. The floor tilted away and I fell. Bones rattled in my wrists. My knees hit hard, jarring into my hips. My head snapped forward, pulling at my spine.

"Fuck," I said.

"Are you okay?" Angie asked.

I didn't know she was there. I came early so I could try some things without her.

"Leave me alone," I said.

Nastiness burned. Angie crossed her arms on her chest.

"Sorry," I said.

She dropped her bag on the floor. Slowly, I pushed myself up. Angie lifted my chin with her fingers. Silver stars sparkled around her eyes. Gold ran through the brown irises.

"When're you due?" she asked.

Panic flared. I jerked away. I turned my back.

"Come on," Angie said. "We're friends, right?"

Darkness shot through with purple and green eddied like smoke through the room.

"Butter," Angie said. "It's okay."

I found a corner and sank into it. Voices echoes through me.

"She's going to hate me," I said.

"Well," Angie said. "You're kind of fucked-up."

Something cold cut along my scalp.

"But I didn't," I said.

Angie laughed. It was a cruel, hard sound, like glass cutting away flesh.

"You're pregnant," she said. "Even Tayla's not that good."

I couldn't look at her, so I closed my eyes. I couldn't breathe so I bit my lip. Blood rolled slowly over my tongue.

"I didn't cheat," I said.

Angie just shook her head.

"I didn't," I said. "I swear."

"The whole virgin birth thing is a little over done," she said.

"Never mind."

I pushed past her. I grabbed my bag and started for the door.

"Who was it?" Angie asked. "It had to be someone, Butter. Even you're not that crazy."

Something hard stopped me. Something tight grabbed hold of me.

"Gid," I said.

Nothing for a long time. Just silence and thought and pity. When she spoke, Angie's voice was laced with ice.

"Jesus," she said.

"Angie," I said. "Please."

"I swear."

She came up behind me and wrapped her arms around my waist.

"Butter," she said. "Even you know better than that."

My spine slumped.

"Tayla's going to lose her mind," Angie said.

"I know."

We sat on the floor together for a long time before she took my hand.

"Shit happens," she said. "Mistakes and whatnot."

It felt as if my skin were going to give away. I was turning into a puddle. Nothing held me together.

"When're you due?" she asked again.

"I don't know."

"You don't know?"

"I can keep it quiet until I start showing."

"You're showing now."

"Jesus."

"You should've had the abortion already."

"I'm keeping it."

"You're keeping it?"

"Tayla and me."

"This isn't Tayla's kid," Angie said. "She's not going to want anything to do with it."

I nodded.

"Adoption?" she asked.

"I don't know."

Angie kissed my forehead.

"Honey," she said, "you need to figure some shit out."

"Yeah," I said.

Time pressed on me, heavier than air or water, heavier than the whole world, not heavy enough to kill me.

A Moment on the Corner

Sunlight broke through clouds gathered like piles of raw wool. It cut through trees beginning to curl with new leaves. The corner was busy. This was where I nearly died. Cars growled and hissed on the wet asphalt. Windows in shops shined with greasy rainbows. No one paid me any mind. I was invisible to everyone but Gid.

He came up behind me and put his hand flat on my belly.

"This lasts forever," he said.

I nodded.

"There's no coming back," he said.

"I know."

Even in the bright light of day, things were cold. My fingers lost their blood and turned white. My feet were too heavy to lift.

"I'll be right here," he said.

"Go away."

I refused to look at him. There was nothing there to see anyway. His face was always lost to me. His hands, his chest, I knew too well. He had nothing I wanted.

"Love lasts forever," he said. "Nothing changes that."

All I had to do was take a step. If I timed it right, no one else would be hurt. It would be an accident.

"There are no accidents," Gid said.

"This whole thing is an accident."

He laughed.

"I chose you," he said. "You chose me."

"No."

"Absolutely."

A logging truck roared past. That was my chance. Something that big would never stop in time. Something that big would finish the job.

"They did nothing to you," Gid said. "Is this a memory you want to leave people?"

Shame and guilt stole my resolve.

"There's nothing to be afraid of," he said.

"Tayla."

The wind whispered small prayers in the trees.

"Yes," Gid said. "Tayla."

When I turned away, he was gone. No one looked at me. I was just another girl walking on the street. No one knew how close I'd come to dying. No one knew what I was thinking.

No Gray

Queertopia was empty but the cafeteria was not. I sat alone in a room full of folks all talking at once. Some of them glanced at me but none of them said anything. Dance Team girls giggled, reeking of laughter and cruelty. Jocks flexed and preened for them. Coy and his gang of fools sat on the far side of the room, heads together, probably planning some kind of off color prank. I watched everyone, and no one watched me.

People scared me. They walked in the halls. They gathered in clumps. I thought of them as clots. Mostly they did no harm. Sometimes, though, broke free and something bad happened. There was no telling what they were going to do. There was no telling what they were going to say.

I watched the room. I watched the familiar and the unfamiliar. I watched everyone fighting and laughing like monkeys let loose from the trees. Tayla came and wrapped her arm around me. She laid her forehead against my jaw.

"You there?" she asked.

I forced a smile. Soon, I was going to have to tell her about the baby. Soon, things were going to change and I tried to imagine my life after. There was nothing there for me. I could take Coy up on his offer. I could go to the clinic and have the doctors there scrape me clean, but then I would have to wear the mark of their scalpels for the rest of my life. I would carry the secret of deliberately killing my baby into the night. Tayla would never know. For the rest of my life, there would be a part of me she knew nothing about. It would rise like an ice wall between us, not entirely impenetrable, but flawed enough to see nothing but warped images.

Gid came and sat at the end of the table, hazy and blurred. Seeing him brought out a sigh.

"Are you okay?" Tayla asked.

I smiled a fake smile. Tayla watched me. Iridescent flickers buzzed around her head like hummingbirds. Her thoughts pushed against me, wordless but heavy, blunt as stones.

"You can tell me," she said.

I shook my head. This secret was mine. This pain was private.

"She's going to leave," Gid said.

"I know."

Tayla turned my face to her with a finger.

"What's going on?" she asked.

"What?"

"Tell her," Gid said.

"No."

"Are you okay?" Tayla asked.

I opened my mouth but there was nothing there but air.

"This is what it's about," Gid said.

"He's back," I said.

Tayla looked around.

"Gid," I said.

Lines went deep in Tayla's face.

"We have to do something," she said.

I nodded.

"This is getting bad," she said.

"I know."

She had no clue. For Tayla, things were either real or not real. There was no middle ground. There was no gray.

Race

Haven was all movement and color. Lasers cut the room to ribbons. Strobes painted everything silver. Music that was barely music thumped and thundered from huge speakers. Monsters made of smoke and light billowed out of the corners, forming and unforming into the crowded dance floor. They reached for me with sharp, misty claws. People hopped and ground themselves into a mass of wriggling hips and shoulders. Miss Tris and Tad shared a chair. Their hands found every corner and crevice in their bodies.

I tried to watch everyone and everything all of the time. Whenever people got too close, I twitched. My gut rose into my throat.

Tayla pinched her eyes together. Her lips looked blue. It might have been the light. It might have been the pressure of too many voices raised in too many conversations. She looked at me and I looked her. She stood and held a hand out. I took it.

"Where you going?" Miss Tris asked.

I shook my head.

"Home," Tayla said.

"It's early," Miss Tris said.

"Yeah," Tayla said.

She plowed a path through the crowd. No one noticed us at all. Miss Tris followed.

"I thought we were going to have fun," she said at the door.

"This isn't fun," Tayla said.

Miss Tris flinched. No one meant to hurt anyone.

"Not my thing," I said.

Miss Tris looked from me to Tayla, from Tayla to the door. "I'm sorry," she said. "Let me get Tad."

She turned. Even from behind, she looked disappointed.

"We can take the bus," I said.

Tayla looked at me.

"Really," I said. "They can stay."

Tayla kissed me. She was gentle heat on my lips. Her hand in mine was the stone on which I built my reality.

When Miss Tris brought Tad, they wore blank faces. This was what they did for fun. Tayla and I were more homebound. We didn't do crowds. We didn't do Euro dance music. Miss Tris started to get into her coat but Tayla stopped her. She handed Tad the keys.

"Drop it off in the morning," Tayla said.

Tad's eyes got big. Tayla wasn't the generous type. Her car was her car. She loaned it to no one.

"You sure?" Tad asked.

"We'll ride the bus," I said.

Miss Tris didn't look convinced.

"I'll be fine," I said.

We stood there like it was big thing for a long time.

It's just a fucking car, I thought.

"I'm tired," I said.

Miss Tris looked at Tad.

"Be careful," Tayla said.

Outside, the night was wet and the streets were loud. Small maple trees stood like gnarled old men along the curb. I stopped, lost for a minute.

"This way," Tayla said.

Clubbers went from door to door dressed in bright colors, done up in too much makeup. To me, it seemed as if clowns had invaded. I giggled a little. Tayla looked at me.

"We don't fit in here," I said.

"No," Tayla said.

"A couple of stodgy old dykes," I said.

We reached the corner and an old man bumped into me.

"Now you'll see what it means," he said.

I turned, confused, a little afraid. But there was no old man, just the pretty people popping from party to party.

"What?" Tayla asked.

I shook my head. A woman in black blocked my way. I jerked against Tayla's hand.

"She's going to find out," the woman said.

I twitched and the woman vanished.

"Butter?" Tayla asked. "What's going on?"

I spun in place.

"Hey," Tayla said. "Talk to me."

"You didn't see her?" I asked.

Tayla's face hardened.

"She was right there," I said.

Down the street, a man screamed.

"Praise be!" he screamed. "The Lord is coming!"

I saw the color of the voices whispering to him. I saw his fear and his joy. I saw the angels wrestling with the demons around him.

"Butter," Tayla snapped. "Look at me."

Her face twisted in the light from the street lamps. A wooden feeling punched into my chest. This was not good. This was a forever moment, when the never ending now threatened to wrap me in dark madness. Cramps formed in my shoulders and thighs. I curled into myself a little.

"Butter," she said. "Let's go home."

I nodded. Tayla dug in her purse and brought out a pill. Ativan.

"Here," she said.

I swallowed it dry and waited.

"You okay?" she asked.

"No," I said.

She pulled me close.

"I'm right here," she said.

The man down the street turned to me.

"Tell her," he said. "Tell her now."

I closed my eyes.

"Let's go," I said.

Tayla pulled me down the sidewalk. I wanted her to go faster. I wanted to see if we could outrun the shit happening in my head. I wanted to see if shame and fear could beat me in a foot race.

Confession

Sleep abandoned me to the night and the night was long. Nausea twisted me into a miserable knot. I lay in bed listening to Tayla mutter. She was prone to nightmares and sometimes the nightmares leaked into the real world. A siren called from somewhere. Mr. Rothgery's dog howled in sympathy.

I tried to be still as possible. Moving brought on the vomiting. Not moving let it sit in the middle of me like a bag of snakes, wriggling and writhing. The room spun and the darkness pressed on me, a layer of sweat and cramps.

When I couldn't hold my stomach in place anymore, I stumbled into the bathroom and crawled into the shower. Hot water made me less sick. Hot water washed away the misery. Time was a trickle of stones rolling over my bones.

I curled in the tub, praying to God to either heal me or let me die. He did neither. Gid whispered at me. He told me that I needed to tell Tayla about the baby. I didn't want to say anything as long as there was a chance, things would change. I thought if I went with Coy to the doctor, the nausea, the agony of keeping secrets, would slip away. But I couldn't bring myself to do anything with Coy.

"This baby is changing things," Gid said. "You are no longer who you were."

I shook my head.

"Together," Gid said. "We will last forever."

The water went cold. I twisted off the stream and stumbled out of the tub. My foot slipped but I caught myself and then it occurred to me that I could have let myself fall. If I fell just right, maybe the baby would come loose. I didn't fall though and I didn't have it in me to drop on my own.

Out in the bedroom, Tayla waited for me. She sat in the bed, eyes dark and swollen. Her hands picked at the blanket and she frowned like something sour had coated her tongue.

"What's up?" she asked.

"Tell her," Gid said.

"Butter?" Tayla asked.

I stood in the doorway, dizzy and weak. I couldn't keep this secret anymore. Words rose like chunks of metal and I swallowed them again only to have them rise all over. I stood and I stared at Tayla and I stared at Gid who stood in the corner.

"Tell her," he said.

I shook my head.

"What's going on?" Tayla asked.

"I'm pregnant."

Fire crossed her face. Her lips thinned to narrow white lines. Even in the dark, I saw the blood drain from her face.

"What?" she asked.

"I'm having a baby," I said.

She stared hard at me, as if she could see right through my flesh at the shadow behind me.

"What does that mean?" she asked.

"I don't know."

"You cheated?" she asked.

"Only in my dreams," I said.

Tayla got out of bed and came to me. She put her face next to mine.

"Details," she said.

"I…"

"Who?" she asked. "How?"

"I don't know."

Her hand came up and I thought she was going to hit me.

"I'll be downstairs," she said and turned away. That was exactly what I was afraid she'd do. I was terrified she would turn away and never turn back.

Silence

Six days of silence.

I woke alone, but not alone. Gid waited by the window, silent, but heavy. The lines of his body were blurred like spilled wine more every day.

"Go away," I said.

Nothing.

"You've done enough," I said.

More nothing.

Getting out of bed was an exercise in strength. The air pressed on me like a hand. Light cut into my eyes like wooden darts. My feet were too heavy, too far away to listen to anything I had to say. I reached for Tayla's hip before I remembered she slept on the couch now. Sighing, refusing to cry, I stumbled out from under the blankets.

Loneliness echoed in the shower. Every drop of water raised a pinpoint of anxiety. I sucked steam into struggling lungs. Gid stood in the misty room watching.

"You need to leave," I said.

"You chose me," he said. "This is your life."

"Not anymore," I said.

I dressed. I walked into the living room. Tayla lay on the couch, her back to the room, wrapped in her rage. I watched her for a moment, trying to come up with the words to make this all okay. There weren't any. She would stay or go on her own. Our life changed. We were no longer a team. We were two pieces of a broken puzzle.

Giving up, I went to the kitchen. Sunlight shined through the thick windows, telling lies. There was no warmth or comfort here. There was distance and space. I cooked the last of the oatmeal. We were broke again. I sweetened it with honey and left it on the table for Tayla. The thought of eating turned my stomach.

I smoked and waited. Tayla came and looked at the cereal for a moment before turning away. Neither of us knew what to do so we did what we always did. We got in the car and went to school.

The ride was awkward and silent. No music. Windows rolled up tight. Road noise the only noise between us.

At school, she parked the car and walked away without even looking at me. I was bigger now, heavier, slower. Without Tayla, there was no grace in me. I shuffled from class to class, silent and sullen. Even Coy knew better than to start things.

At lunch, I was the first one to Queertopia and I waited to see if Tayla would come but she didn't. Tad and Miss Tris came though, and they knew something was up.

"Must be some fight," Miss Tris said.

"Stop," Tad said.

"What?"

"It's none of our business."

I watched for Tayla, but she never showed. I sat there, not eating, trying to figure out a way to make Tayla forgive me. I had to make her understand. I didn't cheat. I needed Tayla to understand that I didn't want to fuck Gid. Gid fucked me. I had nothing to do with it.

"Have you seen her?" I asked.

"In English," Miss Tris said.

I'd seen Tayla then too, but she wouldn't even look at me. She pretended I'd disappeared. Gid followed me through the day, rubbing his hand on my belly, kissing my neck. I tried to act as if he weren't there but he was. He was there, and I was miserable.

"What happened?" Miss Tris asked.

I shook my head.

"Something happened," she said. "Something bad."

She stared at me, but I had nothing to say. It was none of her business. I didn't need the only friends I had left to hate me.

"I need a smoke," I said and got up to go to the Shack.

Miss Tris and Tad followed me. Wind still edged with the smell of snow from the mountains cut through the spaces in the walls. I shivered.

"You have to talk to her," Tad said.

"She thinks I cheated," I said.

Tad and Miss Tris blinked.

"Did you?" Tad asked.

I shook my head.

"Why does she think you did then?" Miss Tris asked.

"Something happened."

They waited for me to tell them the story, but there was no story to tell. We smoked until the bell rang. Miss Tris and Tad ground out their cigarettes and started for the door. I couldn't bring myself to move.

"You coming?" Miss Tris asked.

"Later."

They went in and Gid sighed.

"She will never love you like I do," he said.

"I know."

That was the problem. No one would ever love me the way Tayla did. I wasn't sure I wanted anyone to love me the way Tayla loved me. I wanted Tayla but it seemed like she wanted nothing to do with me.

Waiting

  I danced. I danced and hoped the dance would knock the baby out of me. I danced and sweated and hoped it would bring back something I lost.
  Angie circled me like a cat. She arced and stretched. She was all long lines and sex. Hard muscles in her back and belly felt like smooth stone. The bones in her arms and legs were strong as ancient oak. The music was gentle, too gentle. I needed something to push at. Anger and frustration needed noise. They needed screaming fiddles and groaning bass. I needed something hard to pound against.
  Angie came and together we flew. She was the feather. I was the muscle. We danced until spots bloomed black in the corners. Gid watched. I ignored him.
  When the song ended, when the dance was over, Angie watched me.
  "I can take you home," she said.
  I nodded and gathered my things.
  Angie's car was a box of money made from sex. Her whole life she sold sex without actually fucking anyone. She was perfect in her yoga pants and sports bra. I hated her more than a little. It wasn't her fault but still.
  "Are you still sick?" she asked.
  "Sick?"
  She didn't look at me. She knew and I knew what she was talking about. Part of me hated that she knew about the baby. This was something between Tayla and me. Gid too. It was a wall needing to be climbed. Only I didn't know where to start. There was nothing to take hold of.
  Angie wasn't judging. She was only asking a question.
  "A little," I said.
  "Tayla's a mess," she said.
  "I know."

"Have you talked to her?"

"She won't let me."

Angie nodded. Her face stayed smooth and carefree. "Maybe you need to make her," she said.

"How?"

"You guys know everything about each other," she said. "Just sit her down."

Sitting Tayla down was never a thing I was good at. Tayla never sat for anyone. How was I supposed to make her listen? Tayla only heard what Tayla wanted to hear.

"Is she leaving?" I asked.

Angie shook her head.

"She hasn't said anything to me."

I was terrified that I would come home one night and Tayla would be gone, afraid she'd packed her shit and left. She hadn't left yet though. Maybe she was waiting for something. I only wished I knew what it was.

The Talk

"What's his name?" Tayla asked.
"Tayla…"
"His name!"
"Gid," I said.
"Jesus."
"I told you…"
"He's not real," she said.
"Real enough."
"You want me to believe you're knocked up," she said. "A ghost knocked you up?"
"He's not a ghost."
"Hallucination."
"He's more than that."
"He's not," she said. "No one's ever seen him…"
"I've seen him."
"What's he look like?"
"I don't know."
"You don't know?"
"Tall," I said. "Strong."
"His eyes?"
"I've never seen his eyes."
"Never seen his eyes?"
"His face."
"Jesus."
"Exactly."
"You've never seen his face," she said. "But he knocked you up?"
"It's the only answer."
"Bullshit."
"I've never fucked anyone but you," I said.

"But now," she said, "now you come to me and tell me you're pregnant."

"I didn't fuck him."

"Obviously you did."

"He fucked me," I said.

"Right."

"I'm telling you…"

"I'm telling you," she said. "Somehow, somewhere, you fucked someone and now you want me…you want me to take you back. You and a baby."

"I was thinking adoption," I said.

"I was thinking abortion."

"I can't."

"You can't?"

"No."

"What do you want from me?"

"I don't know."

"So, you're not going to tell me his name?"

"I've told you his name."

"Bullshit."

"Tayla…"

"I don't know what to do."

"Stay."

"I don't know."

"Please."

"We'll see."

Almost a Victim

I sat on the floor and I stared out the window at the trees on the other side of the glass. Sometimes, a car would come around the corner. The lights would push through the shades, painting skeletal lines on the walls.

There were faces here. They snarled and snapped, and I shivered. Purple strings arced into a ceiling shot through with the sickly greens and yellows of old bruises. I needed to puke. I needed to do something. I had to move.

I walked. Dark windows. Moths fluttered in the shadows. I walked and smoked, and I waited to die. My voices told me that the next corner would be a crime scene. They told me that on the next corner, I would die. I pushed forward anyway. If I were to die now, all the grief would evaporate, all the questions would be answered.

When I got to the corner, I waited. No one came. A cat stopped in the middle of the street and stared at me. I lit a cigarette. I watched the fire. In an hour, the sun would be up. In an hour, Tayla would open her eyes and she would stare at me and she would say nothing. Silence, heavy and thick and dark, would stand between us.

I turned away. I started home, upset with my voices for lying about my death. A car careened over the curb, screeching to a stop. A tire blew. Metal sparked against the concrete. The world flashed white and blue. My heart jumped. Had I waited ten seconds, the car would've crushed me. Had I waited ten seconds, the voices would have been right.

It was how things worked in my life, ten seconds off, ten seconds between being a victim and a witness.

Disturbed

Even the echoes died in the halls. Servers and janitors rattled around, some of them whispering in Spanish as if they were afraid of getting in trouble for speaking their native tongue. The cafeteria was empty, and I sat by myself in Queertopia watching the light fall dusty through the windows. I had nowhere to go and nothing to do, so I sat and worried and wondered what the rest of my life was going to look like. Mr. Skarey found me all alone and tried to pry into my life.

"You okay?" he asked.

I shrugged.

"What's up?" he asked.

I shook my head.

"Where is everyone?" he asked.

"Out."

Silence fell for a moment, but then he sat with me thoroughly convinced his presence was not only wanted but needed. He seemed to think he had the answers to whatever questions I had.

But he didn't. No one did. I mean, how was I supposed to go on living when the one girl I loved wouldn't talk to me? How was I supposed to go home when I might find that Tayla had given up all hope and moved out? A baby was coming, and it was coming out of nowhere. I had no idea how I was going to raise a child and even less of an idea if I wanted to.

"You seem disturbed," Mr. Skarey said.

"Aren't we all?" I asked.

"You know what I mean."

I thought for a moment of what I wanted to say to him to make him go away. I wanted to be alone. Even the voices in my head were respecting my need for silence, but here this guy was pushing his fingers into my pie and I found myself wanting to tell him everything.

"I'm pregnant," I said, and I watched his face struggle to stay smooth, non-judgmental.

"Aren't you…"

"Yes."

Confession stopped him up for a second. He swallowed, and he blinked too much too fast.

Questions flickered over his face.

"Is the father . . .?" he asked. "Do I know him?"

I shook my head.

"Is there something I should know?" he asked.

"It's just a guy," I said. "He doesn't go to school."

"Is there anything I can do?" he asked. "I mean, to help?"

I shrugged.

"I need it to be over," I said.

Silence slithered over us. He waited for me to say something more, but there was nothing more to say. When it was clear the conversation was over, he rose and leaned in close.

"You know where to find me," he said.

"Absolutely."

"Good."

He stood there for a second before smiling like everything was going to be okay and walking away. I listened to his shoes slap the linoleum floor. It was time to go home. It was time to see what else could go wrong.

Nothing Changed

Cherry blossoms came apart in the wind, pink and white petals twisting in the air before settling on cars, gathering in gutters, sticking to windows. Cigarette smoke hung for a moment in the air before falling apart. I felt sick. Something stuck to the back of my throat, gagging me. I choked on the very air.

Down behind the greenhouse, stoners got stoned. Out in the parking lot, skinny chicks and geeks shuffled into school. I didn't fit in. I had nothing in common with these people. Miss Tris and Tad showed up in pink. They laughed and joked until they saw me and not Tayla.

Things were getting awkward with everyone.

"You look miserable," Tad said.

"I am."

"What's up?" Miss Tris asked.

"Things," I said.

I thought for a moment. It was time to talk. They needed to know. I knew they worried about me and I knew they worried about Tayla. They just didn't know what was happening or why.

"I have something to tell you," I said.

I stopped for a moment and put the words together in my head before letting them fall to my mouth and out into the world. My skin crawled and sweat sprung out all over.

"Guys," I said. "Tayla and I…I'm pregnant."

It hung there for a moment.

"How'd that happen?" Miss Tris asked.

"Don't know," I said.

"Jesus," Tad said.

"No kidding."

The bell rang but none of us moved. This was more important than class. They had questions just like everyone else. Only, with these guys, I was willing to answer some of them.

"So that's why Tayla's all bent," Tad said.

"She thinks I cheated," I said.

"Well…" Miss Tris said.

"It was Gid," I said.

"The guy from your dreams?" Tad asked.

"Exactly."

Disbelief and pity fought for dominance. They frowned and thought and tried to not seem too judgmental.

"I didn't cheat," I said.

"You did something," Tad said.

"It's not like that."

"What's it like then?" Tad asked.

"I didn't want this."

"No doubt," Miss Tris said.

"There's just one way to get pregnant," Tad said.

"I swear," I said. "I didn't fuck anyone."

A swirling wind lifted a few petals in the air.

"It doesn't matter," Miss Tris said. "We love you. It doesn't change anything."

They came and hugged me and the weight of their arms brought me back from the edge of madness for a moment. Now all I had to do was figure out how to get Tayla to believe me too.

Spark

All night, I sat in the living room watching Tayla sleep. All night, voices shouted threats and commands. They told me people's lives would be easier if I were dead. They told me people would be happier. I was a sinful, ugly, fat girl. I had no business breathing. All night, I listened to them and wondered what the world would be like without me.

Shadows formed ugly masks in the dim light from the street. They fell from the walls like pebbles into a bucket. They shattered on the floor and grew in gnarled, ash-colored lines back to the ceiling, starting the whole thing over. Their raw, hideous teeth gnawed at my sanity. Breathing was hard, shallow and sharp. My ribs hurt. My eyes watered.

Tayla lay on her side on the couch, her hair falling over her face, leaving her narrow eyes dark. Sometimes, she whistled through her teeth. It made me smile that I could sit there watching her without her ever knowing it. It was the only time in a long time that her face wasn't pinched with anger and grief.

"She'll never understand," Gid said.

He stepped out of the shadows. Light lined the edges of his body like a pale halo. I closed my eyes and pretended he wasn't there. I imagined that for a moment. I didn't want to feel the jagged edge of his voice. I didn't want him touching me. But he did. He touched me. His cold fingers stroked the line of my collarbone and I felt sick.

"Go away," I said.

"I love you," he said.

His too sweet breath rolled over my face like jasmine climbing a lattice. His burning lips marked my neck, the line of my jaw. Blood rushed out of me. I imagined looking at him, looking at his bloody face and for once knowing what he looked like.

"You're not real," I said.

"You know better."

Suddenly, I was angry. I burned and twitched and all I wanted was to scream but I didn't scream. People were sleeping and this was between Gid and me. This was a private battle.

"You've ruined everything," I said.

"You'll rebuild," he said.

No matter what I did, he wouldn't leave. There was no escape. If I lived, he lived. If I breathed, he breathed. Suicide suddenly became much more reasonable. I mean, Tayla had kept me alive this long and now I wasn't sure she'd even be there in the morning. I stayed up all night just to keep her from sneaking away without telling me. Now she was gone. Not gone, gone but gone as in silent and distant. Being around her was like cutting myself open with a glass knife.

Gid came close. He was going to kiss me. I couldn't stand the thought of that, so I reached for his face. He spun away. I reached again.

"Don't," he said.

His voice was thinner than usual, sharp enough to cut the air between us.

"I need to know," I said.

He stepped back. He raised his hands.

"You cannot know this," he said.

"It's going to happen," I said. "Someday. Soon."

"No."

He faded. Not even his voice lingered. It was little thing. Little but enough to spark a little light, a little hope.

Reunion

First thing in the morning, I found a note in my locker. No one ever left notes in my locker. When I saw it, I thought maybe Tayla had left it. I knew better, I hoped. We hadn't said anything to each other for weeks. Maybe, I thought, this was her way of trying to get past things.

I opened the note and on it was written: *The offer stands. Coy. PS: You're starting to show.*

I closed my eyes. Coy was the last person I wanted to hear from. Life was so much easier when he was nothing more than an aggravation and a pain in the ass. This solicitousness complicated things. Of course, he couldn't just be nice. He offered a kindness but backed it up with a slam.

I folded the note and tucked it into my pocket. No one needed to know that I was talking to Coy. It would piss people off. Miss Tris and Tad would never understand and Tayla would just walk away. I needed her to walk closer.

Walking down the hall, I watched for people staring at my belly. I kept one hand on it, pushing, hoping no one knew what I carried there. My belly was still hard and flat, and no one said anything. No one seemed to stare at me more than usual.

In bio, I stared out the window. Off and on, Gid's face reflected there. Off and on, the teacher's voice cut through the white noise in my head. I wanted to go home, but there was nothing there for me, so I wandered through the day, watching people, worrying about what was coming next.

At lunch, in Queertopia, Tayla came and sat with us. Tad and Miss Tris tried not to stare, but their eyes washed over us on and off. Tayla ignored them. She ate and she kept her face down over her plate. I wanted to touch her. My fingertips ached with a wild desire to feel her jaw's soft line.

"So," she said. "Gid?"

I nodded.

"You know," she said, "no one's going to believe you."

"I know."

"Gid," she said.

"He's the only one."

She closed her eyes. She closed her eyes and she breathed and then she put her hand on my knee. Fire jerked through the muscles there.

"I...," she said and sighed. "It's hard."

This was it. This was the first step. Doubt still stained her voice, but she was willing to consider the possibility I wasn't lying. Maybe she'd come back to bed now. Maybe she'd tell me what I needed to do to make this real to her.

Back in my Bed

Three faces hung in the corners, pale and swollen, tongues hanging like slugs from their thick lips. I sat in my bed feeling sick. I wanted sleep. I needed it but I couldn't. Voices scraped along my jaw bone telling me over and over that Coy was coming through the window with a knife to kill me.

I sat with my knees tucked under my chin and tried to act as if I were alone. Laughter crawled through the room. Something fluttered in my belly. It could have been the baby or it could have been gas.

I couldn't take it anymore and went downstairs. I went downstairs and found Tayla lying on the couch asleep. I sat at her feet and waited for her to wake. Headlights from the street lit up the curtains over the window. Tayla started rustling, batting at some dream. Her eyes ran circles in their sockets. After a moment, she woke. Surprise blanched her face.

"What?" she asked.

I said nothing. I just watched her face, her swollen eyes and pale lips.

"Butter?" she asked.

"Can't sleep," I said.

Tayla sat up. She sat up and stretched.

"What's going on?" she asked.

"Too much."

She knew what I mean when I said that. She'd been with me through too much in the past not to know what I meant.

"She hates you," Gid said, his voice coming from the walls, the air.

Part of me believed him. Part of me nearly got up and left. But then part of me knew that she loved me. She's loved me since the seventh grade.

"Gid?"

"No," I said. "Yes. And others."

"I need a cigarette," Tayla said.

She stumbled into her clothes and we went out to the patio. Sunrise was hours away. School was hours away. No one moved in the night. It still felt as if someone were watching me but having Tayla there helped. Tayla made me feel safe. Tayla made this world, the physical world more genuine than the world in my head.

"You're okay," Tayla said.

"Yeah?"

"Nothing's going to happen," she said. "I'm right here."

"I need you."

She looked at the gnarled and twisted trees. She looked into the shadows at the edge of the yard.

"I need time," she said.

"I thought…"

"It's hard."

I nodded. I nodded and finished my smoke.

"Would it be better if I lay down with you?" she asked.

"You don't have to."

"I know," she said.

I closed my eyes. She had no idea how nice it would be to have her in my bed again. She had no idea how nice it would be to feel her pressed against my spine, protecting me from the villains in my dreams, the intrusion of unwanted visitors.

Far From Perfect

Antiseptic walls rose from a tile floor. White cabinets hung pure and bland. Acoustic panels sucked the noise from the room. In the corner, the ultrasound machine waited for me. I lay on the exam table counting my breaths. Tayla held my hand.

No voice. No faces. No Gid.

The tech did her thing. My hands shook. I nearly puked.

"It's not going to hurt," she said.

Her hands were warm and strong when they lifted my shirt. It was hard to tell if my belly was bigger, rounder than yesterday or last week. I closed my eyes and waited.

"I'm right here," Tayla said.

"That's the heartbeat," she said.

A rapid flutter on the screen echoed the high pitched thunder from the speakers.

"Jesus," Tayla said.

I closed my eyes. I didn't want to see the heartbeat. I didn't want to hear it. This wasn't possible.

"A miracle," the tech said, smiling like she knew things.

"You don't know," Tayla said, a little edgy.

The tech frowned for a moment but said nothing.

"There's a hand," she said.

I turned away.

"Are you okay?" the tech asked.

Tears soaked into the paper under my shoulders.

"She's just emotional," Tayla said.

Doubt shaded the tech's face.

"Are you sure?" she asked.

Tayla's voice got all protective.

"This isn't easy," she said.

The tech said nothing for a while.

"It's okay," Tayla said.

"It's real," I said.

"I know."

Her fingers squeezed mine.

"Look," she said.

When I opened my eyes, the tech stared at me, concerned, a little scared maybe.

"Don't ask," I said.

For a moment, I thought she was going to ignore me and ask anyway but then she nodded.

"Sorry," she said.

"It's okay."

She moved from hand to head, from head to spine.

"Do you want know the sex?" she asked.

"His name is Adam," Gid said out of nowhere.

"It's a boy," I said.

She looked startled and the conviction in my voice.

"How do you know?" Tayla asked.

I looked at her, the answer in my eyes.

"Oh," she said.

"Well," the tech said, too cheerful. "Everything looks good."

"Really?" I asked.

"Perfect," she said.

I shook my head. "I'm seventeen," I said. "This is far from perfect."

Fair

Angie stood in the middle of the room. Anger painted her face fierce white, hints of pink.

"No," she said.

"Why?"

"This is not an argument," she said.

Tayla stood by the door looking a little out of place.

"I'm fine," I said.

"You're pregnant," Angie said.

"Yeah."

"Talk to me after," she said.

"Angie…"

"No."

She grabbed her bag and started for the door.

"This might be what you want," she said. "But I'm not going to help you be stupid."

She stopped when she saw Tayla.

"Talk to her," I said.

Tayla lifted her hands.

Angie touched her face.

"Glad to see you," she said.

Tayla smiled.

"Take care of her," Angie said.

"Okay," Tayla said.

I kicked my bag across the room. Angie left and Tayla waited.

"I have to do something," I said.

"I know."

"Fuck," I said.

"Things change," Tayla said.

"It's not fair!"

Tayla laughed. I glared at her.

"Don't talk to me about fair," she said.

That put an end to it.

Face

I walked in sunlight. It tasted of spring. In the yards I passed purple crocus pushed out of black soil. Robins and ravens cut patterns in the sky. I walked in the sunlight at the end of the day. I walked, and I smoked cigarettes and I thought about things.

In my belly, the baby danced. It started as a flutter and grew into a whole routine. He pushed against my ribs. Gid came out of the trees wrapped in burgundy light and pressed his hands to my belly. They were heavy and ugly hands and I wanted nothing to do with him. But he was there, and he felt our child moving.

"Active," Gid said.

"Don't," I said.

He laughed, and he walked with me, a shade darker than the shadows falling from the trees.

"I need something," I said. "I need to see your face."

I'd been thinking of this for a while. Whenever I tried to see his face, whenever I tried to touch the line of his jaw or the plane of his cheek, he disappeared. It gave me a thought.

"My face," Gid said, "is unimportant."

I turned away and he shuddered a little in the sunlight. I made him uncomfortable now. It was kind of nice. I had no reason to make him comfortable. He did nothing to make me comfortable. He came, and he took what he wanted when he wanted. He thought nothing of me or how I might feel. After everything he'd done to me, I felt like pushing him into a corner and peeling away the blurred light covering everything. Something told me that seeing Gid's face would save my life. Something told me that this was how I was going to be free.

"What will our son look like?" I asked.

"You'll know," he said, "in time."

We walked, and my place came up. The sun rushed into the mountains.

"What happens," I asked, "if I see your face?"

"Everything ends," he said.

"Everything?"

"Everything."

I shook my head. Everything would end. Everything. What an interesting thought. I stopped and grabbed at him. Thick arms pushed me away. The lines around him distorted. His broad chest turned translucent. I saw the world through him for a moment.

"Stop," he said, sharp and angry.

"No."

Retreating, turning away, he faded.

"So, this is it," I said. "This is how it ends."

"You chose me," he said, his voices thinning.

"No."

"You see me," he said. "You need me."

"I don't want you."

"I need you."

His voice now was simple a sigh.

"Not my problem," I said.

When he'd completely retreated into memory and nothingness, I smiled. I was winning. Finally, I knew things. I knew how to end this nightmare.

Names

Lunch came and we all sat in Queertopia with our half-cooked burritos and our laughter, Miss Tris and Tad, Tayla and me. We chattered on about the Dance Team girls and the stupid shit we were learning in class. We told stories of the pain in the ass teachers and made plans for the weekend. Everyone seemed to ignore us, and we ignored them. But then things turned serious.

"You have a name yet?" Miss Tris asked.

"Adam," I said.

Tayla raised an eyebrow.

"Adam?" she asked.

"Something wrong with Adam?"

"It's so white bread."

I nodded. Tayla wanted everything to stand out. She wanted everyone around her to know the limits of people's kindness and the boundaries of what was okay and what was not.

"You have no idea," I said. "The shit I went through just because of what my mother called me."

"I get it," Miss Tris said.

Of all my friends, Miss Tris was the one who knew what it was like to be on the outside looking in. Tayla and Tad didn't have to live here. If they kept their mouths shut, no one knew they were different. People only had to look at me to know I didn't fit. I was fat and I was non-descript, and people assumed I had no self-control or self-respect and most of them assumed I was a dyke because God knew that all dykes were fat and all fat girls were dykes. Tayla looked punkish and fierce and people only had to talk to her once to know that she stood in the twilight because she wanted to.

Miss Tris, she started life with a dick and now she had tits. Most of the time, she fit in just right with those of us who didn't care, but even then, born girls didn't trust her because they didn't think she'd ever get over her masculine need to conquer and men didn't trust her because they assumed she wanted to fuck them with the remnants of her boyhood.

"Adam's a good name," I said. "It means Man in Hebrew."

"Man?" Tayla asked.

"Man," I said. "And Gid said…"

"No!" Tayla snapped. "We don't talk about him."

Miss Tris and Tad looked a little lost. They stared at me and Miss Tris shrugged. Tayla turned her face to her plate but she wasn't eating. Something had happened here. Tayla was on the way to getting over the whole baby thing, but she wasn't there all the way.

"I need a smoke," she said and stood, and I stood with her. Miss Tris and Tad followed us to the Shack. Cigarette smoke soon rose like the promises of saints into the air. No one said anything.

"So," Miss Tris said, "do you think the baby's going to be gay?"

We all turned to look at her. Sometimes even someone on the inside said stupid shit.

"Maybe," I said. "If he's not too busy saving the world."

Everyone laughed. Tayla took my hand. Everything was warm for a moment.

"I don't like Adam," she said.

"Gid…"

"Hush," she said. "We'll figure something out. Not Adam though. Gid can kiss my ass."

I nodded. This was our thing. Not his. Nothing mattered except what mattered to us and right now, all that mattered was Tayla holding my hand, talking like she'd come around. It didn't matter if she believed or not. She was here.

Fair Warning

Coy had something to say and he couldn't say it to me. His friends and my friends would have never understood that we had anything to say to each other. They would never understand that we had something in common. So Coy couldn't talk to me at lunch or in class. He couldn't even talk to me in the hallway. Because he had something to say to me, he wrote a note and the note read: *You've decided to keep it. Good for you. Meet me in the gym after school.*

I tossed the note in the trash and waited for Tayla to come find me. She found me at my locker. I waited for her and she came, and she looked at my face.

"Something up?" she asked.

I shook my head.

"Your face says you're lying," she said.

"I have to meet Mr. Skarey after school," I lied.

Tayla looked at me and decided to believe me. I didn't know what she would have thought if I had told her the truth. She was just getting over the whole baby's father thing. She didn't quite believe in Gid but she was willing to let it sit for the moment. I let her let me believe everything was okay.

The rest of the day passed with the slow grind of knowing I was going to have to come up with a reason to send Tayla home without me without her knowing that I'd lied to her. Classes passed like sand over burned skin. I was brittle and nearly broken by the time the last bell rang. Tayla found me.

"I can wait," she said.

"I'm okay."

"You shouldn't have to walk all that way," she said.

"I need to get away," I said. "Just for a moment."

She let me go and walked out to her car. I went to the gym. Echoes played along the cinder block walls. Coy waited for me in the bleachers. The room was empty of anyone but us.

"Have you thought of adoption?" he asked.

"No."

I wasn't happy about the baby, but I wasn't doing anything to get rid of it either. I'd gotten used to the idea. It was my baby.

"I told my mom," he said. "She's thinking about going to the school to make them kick you out until after the baby's born. She's going to try to get them to force you into giving it up."

"It's my baby."

"Dykes have no right to children," he said.

"Fuck you."

I walked away.

"You're too young," he said.

"Old enough."

I was in the hall when Gid found me.

"This is love," he said with his paisley voice. "He knows nothing of love."

"Neither do you," I said, raising a hand.

Gid flinched.

"Show me," I said.

He vanished. I smiled. Control, power over things were new. I liked it. I felt better knowing I could hurt him back.

On the Edge of Things

People talked but they only talked sideways. They took the rumors and the gossip; they took the lies and the half-truths and assumed they had the whole story.

I walked through the halls, bigger than usual. Dance Team girls snickered in the halls. Teachers eyed me with hard eyes. Jocks stopped and stared. I kept my chin tucked to my chest and I kept quiet.

They called me dyke. They called me abomination. They tossed cruel words at me and I took them like darts, flinching only a little.

Jessica Barber stood at my locker. She had a box of things on the floor.

"There you are," she said.

The words were too bright. Jessica was a one of those girls who thought she could say anything if she said it with a smile.

"I have some stuff for you," she said.

She wore a silk shirt over black leggings. Her hips were too narrow. Her shoulders elegant. I hated looking at her.

"Babies need stuff," she said. "Expensive stuff."

Shame rose yellow and sickly in me.

"I know you have troubles," she said.

This was her way of being nice. I didn't trust. Jessica had never had time for me. She was the queen of the chastity pledge, even with a baby of her own. No one looked at her the way they looked at me. If I were a braver girl, I would've told her to kiss my ass. But I wasn't. I was scared. I was fat. I was lonely.

"Diapers and formula," she said.

"Okay."

"You don't want to breast feed," she said. "My mom says it ruins your boobs. Not that that might mean anything to you."

Teeth flashed in her mouth.

"I have some newborn clothes here too," she said. "Nice stuff."

"Okay."

She came forward with her arms wide and wrapped me in a hug.

"I'm so glad you decided to make better choices," she said.

"What?"

Jessica's face, perfect, smooth and made up, looked troubled.

"That Tayla," she said. "She was so bad for you."

A spark of recognition. A moment of clarity.

"I don't need your leftovers," I said.

She smiled again.

"It's okay," she said. "I don't need it."

Tayla came down the hall. When she saw me with Jessica, she stopped; I lifted my hand.

"Tayla and I are in love," I said.

Jessica's eyes got big. Her mouth dropped open for a moment.

"I thought," she said. "I mean you're pregnant."

I nodded.

"Oh," she said.

Thoughts wheeled through her head. She looked at everyone looking at us.

"Go ahead," she said. "Charity's good for the soul."

Awkward and confused, she walked away. Slowly, people went back to ignoring me. Tayla looked from me to the box and back again.

"Pity gifts?" she said.

"Yeah."

We stood silent.

"We kind of need it," I said.

Tayla nodded.

"She thought we broke up," I said.

"Yeah."

The moment got heavy and dark.

"We're okay," I said. "Right?"

Tayla lifted the box.

"Let's go home," she said.

I knew she wanted to throw the box in a dumpster. I knew how hard it was for her to take anything from people like Jessica Barber. We stood on the edge of things. We always would, but sometimes, we had to take the scraps the real people left for us.

Safe

Dead folks filled the room without walls. None of them had faces, only bumps for the nose and pits for their eyes. Their mouths were filled with glass teeth, jagged, sharp and dangerous. I knew them even without their faces. Everyone I knew, had ever known, would ever know was there. They were there and they danced. They circled like dust devils. Waves of rage washed through them. They crashed against me as if I were a stone in a tide.

Soon, their spiky fingers pinched away pieces of me. There was no blood, just meat and pain. I couldn't move. I couldn't fight them off. I couldn't breathe. Mud filled my lungs. I wanted to scream but all I could do was gasp and tremble. When they got to my belly, they cut into me, trying to pull the baby out. My skin healed as fast as they pulled it away. They couldn't get to him.

Gid saved me. He lifted me into the purple sky and we moved without moving. Everything was smooth and iridescent. He took me to the edge of a pit, a pit so deep, so dark; I couldn't begin to comprehend it. Voices lifted out it like an updraft, hot and angry. Pain filled every bit of wind.

"This is yours," he said.

I shook my head.

"This is what waits," he said.

The baby kicked my ribs. I lunged, and my fingertips brushed the point of his chin. Flesh showed for a moment. Bone cracked. For the first time, part of him became human. I lunged again, and he slapped me down. Blood and pain exploded in my face. I fell to the floor.

Everything stopped. Light flared. I opened my eyes.

"You okay?" Tayla asked.

I shook my head.

"Nightmare," she said.

"I was dying," I said.

Her hand squeezed my hand.

"You're fine," she said. "You're safe."
But I wasn't. I couldn't even remember what safe felt like.

Consequences

Mr. Skarey's office was all pale walls and diplomas, as if he were afraid no one would believe him capable of his job without the papers hanging around to prove it. Tayla and I sat in the hard chairs. My back ached. My feet were too big in too small shoes. Silence hung like a hammer in the room. Faces bubbled out of the walls. Voices rode over everything.

Gid came and stood behind me with his purple hands on my shoulders. I shrugged them away.

"How are things?" Mr. Skarey asked, finally.

"What's going on?" Tayla asked.

Mr. Skarey didn't like looking out of control, so he turned a hard eye on her.

"We have a problem," he said.

"A problem?" I asked.

Mr. Skarey squinted and blew his breath through his nose.

"It seems there are students here," he said. "Students who've talked to their parents and their parents have talked to me."

"Jesus," Tayla said.

"Your pregnancy," he said, "seems to offend certain people."

"Fucking Coy," Tayla said.

"Language," Mr. Skarey said.

"What's the problem?" I asked.

"It seems that some folks think it would be better if you transitioned to home school."

Now there it was. It hung in the air and weighed us all down.

"Home school?" I asked.

"Fuck this," Tayla said.

She started to stand but Mr. Skarey held up a hand. Tayla slumped back into her chair.

"Some folks," Mr. Skarey said, "find your pregnancy distracting and a poor example for the rest of the student body."

"Fuck the student body," Tayla said.

"Tayla…" Mr. Skarey said.

"No," she shot back. "People're trying to kick my girlfriend out of school because she's having a baby. It's bullshit."

"We'd send a tutor," Mr. Skarey said.

"What about Jessica Barber?" Tayla asked.

Mr. Skarey turned a little white. Fear maybe. Anger?

"I can't talk about other students," he said.

"Fuck you," Tayla said.

"It's okay," I said.

"No," Tayla said. "It's not."

"I'm afraid there's nothing I can do," Mr. Skarey said.

"You could grow a pair," Tayla said.

"Just as well," Mr. Skarey said. "I'll call you with details."

And that was that. Being gay was fine. Being fat was fine. But being gay and fat and pregnant, that was too much for people to bear.

A Domestic Moment

I lay on the bed and Tayla rested her head on my belly.
"He's kicking," she said.
"I noticed."
"Does it hurt?"
"Sometimes. Most times it's like I need to fart and can't."
"That's funny."
"Yeah."
"I didn't think you knew how to fart."
"I'm discrete."
"Yes, you are," she said.
Sweet feelings circled in my chest. This was a moment I wanted to hold onto.
"I worry," Tayla said.
"I know."
"We have to be careful."
"We are careful."
"People," she said. "People can be vicious."
"Yeah."
 "We'll do our best."
"What if it's not enough?"
"We can only do so much."
"I just want to make sure you're taking the best care of yourself."
"I am taking care of myself."
"You're trying."
"I'm doing more than trying."
Tayla didn't look convinced. I could see the argument in her face, but she swallowed it and nodded.
"Can you believe it's only a few weeks away?" she asked.
"I'm ready."
"Do you regret it?"
"No," I said. "Not really."

The baby hiccupped, a rhythmic dance.
"Are you happy?" I asked.
"I can't remember the last time I was happy."
"I wish I could fix that."

Birth

It started with a rush of water. It started with pain. Contractions threatened to tear me in half. I sat in the living room. Tayla jumped.

"Is that what I think it is?" she asked.

I nodded.

"Son of a bitch!"

"Oh God," I said. "Oh God!"

Tayla rushed around getting shit ready. She grabbed clothes. She helped me out to the car. It was the middle of the night and the lights were all hazy and haloed in the rain. The pain was ridiculous. It was so bad that all I could do was laugh.

The voices and the faces were gone. I stood on the edge of the world and waited for this thing in my belly to claw its way through my middle.

Tayla charged through traffic with no thought to safety or courtesy. No cops stopped us. People blew their horns and Tayla tossed profanities at them like stones.

At the hospital, Tayla got a wheelchair. She rushed me through the doors. A nurse looked up.

"Baby," Tayla said.

The nurse looked confused for a moment then it dawned on her what was happening.

"Did your water break?" the nurse asked.

"Yes."

She strapped an ID bracelet on me and wheeled me into the back. She and Tayla helped me onto an examination table. They put my feet up in stirrups. The nurse checked me.

"Seven centimeters," she said.

"What does that mean?"

"It means you're having a baby today."

A doctor came, and he checked me too.

"You're going to be okay," he said.

Why would he say that? I wasn't worried about being okay until then. They set up an IV and gave me something. I nodded off between contractions. They got closer and closer.

"It hurts."

"I know," the nurse said.

"No, you don't…Jesus."

"Almost there," she said.

"Shut up."

"Slow and easy," she said.

I tried to go slow and easy, but everything was happening too fast. I needed to know what was going on, but everyone was busy doing their things.

"Get a bassinette in here," the doctor said.

The nurse left and came back with a bassinette. Tayla held my hand.

"You're doing fine…"

"Not right now."

"Okay…holy shit"

"Push," said the doctor — so I pushed.

"Again."

I pushed again.

"Again."

And I pushed again.

I felt the baby's head come loose.

"Push," said the doctor.

I pushed, and the shoulders came free. The rest slithered out like an eel. The doctor caught it and immediately handed it off to the nurse.

"You have a little boy," the doctor said.

He helped me clear the placenta and let me doze on the table.

"So little," Tayla said.

When they handed me my son, I cried. This was nothing like I imagined. This was a wild kind of magic no one had ever told me about. I had a son. I was a mother. What next? How was I supposed to do this?

A Comfortable Madness

Middle of the night. Purple air heavy with the smell of lilacs. Tayla and I sat on the patio smoking. The baby slept in the living room.

"Do you think this'll work?" Tayla asked.

I shrugged. Nerves made Tayla antsy. Her eyes darted around the night like mice looking for the door out of a trap.

"This isn't good," Tayla said. "I know he's real. To you. But…"

When Gid came out of the shadows, I was ready for him. He came and he stopped with his back to the porch light. His shoulders were lined with hard, indigo light and his hair hung around his head like a halo.

"There he is," I said.

Tayla's head snapped around.

"I don't," she said. "There's nothing there."

"So," Gid said.

I shook my head. I stood, tall and strong.

"I love you," he said.

"No."

"Butter…" Tayla said.

"No."

I stepped up and I grabbed his chin. His chin was hard and sharp. He jerked away but I grabbed him again. Light flickered. Everything went still, as if the world were waiting to see what was going to happen.

"Son of a bitch," Tayla said, kicking her chair back and nearly toppling over.

"See?" I asked.

"No," Gid said. "She's blind."

"Fuck," Tayla said, terrified.

"Look at me," I said.

He fought with me, but there was a new kind of strength in my hands. I held him tight.

"Stop," he said.

His voice sounded desperate.

"I need you," he said.

I turned his face to the light and there it was. For the first time, I saw him for what he was. He was a man, only a man.

"I'm not like you," he said.

"No one is."

"Please," he said.

I let him go and he stepped away. Tayla came and stood with me.

"It's time for you to go," I said.

"Butter…"

I held up my hand.

"I'm done," I said.

It took a second, but he started to fade. The edges of his body disintegrated. He turned to lavender sparks and vanished in the wind.

"Jesus," Tayla asked. "What the hell?"

I took her hand.

"That was real," she said.

"Told you."

"But what?" she asked. "I mean what…"

"I don't know."

Slowly, things went back to normal. The voices I'd grown up with came back. They were too real, but not real enough. They warned me about the strangers on the street, the murderers on the corner. I closed my eyes. Tayla pulled me close and held tight, standing with me in a comfortable madness.

About the Author

William L. Alton started writing in the Eighties, during a long stay in a state psychiatric hospital. It started with poetry to impress the girls and evolved into a true and complete compulsion. Since then, he has gone on to earn a Bachelor of Arts and a Master of Fine Arts from Pacific University in Forest Grove, Oregon. There he married and raised three boys. He currently lives in Portland and works with at risk teenagers.

Made in the USA
Lexington, KY
27 May 2018